MEN ARE LUNATICS, WOMEN ARE NUTS!

OTHER BOOKS IN THIS SERIES:

MEN ARE LUNATICS, WOMEN ARE NUTS!

WOMEN AND MEN TALK ABOUT MEN AND WOMEN

Compiled and with an introduction
by Ronald B. Shwartz

RUNNING PRESS
PHILADELPHIA · LONDON

To Marisa Jaye Shwartz, a woman in the making, and to her grandmother, Joyce Rosenthal Shwartz, who will help show her the way.

9   8   7   6   5   4   3   2   1
Digit on the right indicates the number of this printing

Library of Congress Cataloging-in-Publication Number 96-67149

ISBN 1-56138-792-4

Cover and interior design by Frances J. Soo Ping Chow
Pictures researched by Susan Oyama
Cover photographs: Super Stock
Interior photographs: H. Armstrong Roberts

This book may be ordered by mail from the publisher.
Please add $2.50 for postage and handling.
But try your bookstore first!

Running Press Book Publishers
125 South Twenty-second Street
Philadelphia, Pennsylvania 19103-4399

Acknowledgments

The author wishes to thank his agent, Sheree Bykofsky; his editor, Tara Ann McFadden; his editorial assistant, Mary Stevenson; and his secretary, Janet Sutton. He also thanks Alison Comey, James Duzak, Deborah Leff, Wendy Harrison, Darline Lewis, and Daniel Sacco, each for different reasons. He also wishes to thank his lucky stars for steering all these people in his direction.

CONTENTS

Introduction

At first, before the dawn of a rude awakening, I thought that all this flapdoodle about men and women was nothing to write home about—much less a book about. Of course, prepubescent lug that I was, I learned early on that women are softer, smell better, live longer, and tend to take salad dressing on the side. And I figured out that women play harder to get, and as a rule play it better than football. Later, but still early on, I heard the more distant rumors: men don't ask directions; women have friends, men only buddies; men live in black and white, women in color; women say "Excuse me" where men simply flip the bird. All told, by the advent of my eighteenth year, I figured that when it came to the opposite sex, I'd been there, done that, that's all she wrote. In short— I didn't have a clue.

It was no secret even to me that men and women could live neither with nor without the other. Still, in the ancient war of the sexes, reports from the front had seemed to me hardly news at all. Little did I know that an uneasy truce had swerved from its familiar course. Soldiers who once slept soundly with the enemy had gone AWOL in unparalleled numbers. The distinctions between yin and yang—always at once elusive and treacherous—were now more confused than ever, the source of a cultural obsession. The new dawn of gender politics.

These days, in fact, the term *opposite sex* seems almost quaintly understated. It implies a symmetry altogether too neat in a world where men and women seem so close yet so far away—just like in boxing, where being "close" doesn't always mean cordial. The word on men, in one corner, is that the good ones are either taken or gay. Men, it is said, gotta do what they gotta do, and having done so, are now known by an overworked litany of zoological epithets, like "swine," "sick puppies," and "rutting weasels." Even the tolerable ones are Neanderthals who dominate conversations, leave toilet seats up, and channel-surf to the point of stupor. Whether exploring their feminine side or their warrior roots, they just don't get it, don't know they need it, and can't help it.

Women, in the other corner, are said to have come a long way—maybe. They have evolved from June Cleaver too fast for some, for others not fast enough, and even the smart ones make foolish choices. Freud by his own account did not know what women want, and it now appears that what women want is for Freud to butt out. If the new oracle of choice happens to be *Seinfeld*, what women want is to buy shoes. Or if it's Cyndi Lauper, they just want to have fun. Or if it's *Thelma and Louise*, they want paybacks. Maybe what they want most is just some warm breathing space between the glass ceilings and false-bottom floors—to simply discover, in such a world, which way is up.

No wonder men and women are walking wounded in a maze of mutual misunderstanding. Somehow the tectonic plates keep shifting. The landscape is still plagued by a groundswell of misogyny, and the specter of sexual harassment, from presidents on down, has the rest of us flirting—if at all—with disaster. What we seem to have here is no mere failure to communicate, or to liberate. No mere gender "gap," but a yawning chasm. What we have, in reality, are the stirrings of a new *Weltschmerz*—and no solution is at hand. If one sex were in fact from Mars and the other from Venus, both could just return to their respective planets and life on Earth could start over—reemerging from primordial ooze to the amoeba level, where coexistence has no border disputes and breaking up is in fact *not* hard to do but is in fact the whole point.

In the world as we know it there's no such luck and no explanation to be had. Maybe it's just the new millennium or some hormonal disharmony touched off by the moon landing. At any rate, this book is a modest attempt to showcase the symptoms and to canvass pop culture, and what remains of the rest of culture, in search of wit and wisdom in both classic and demented form. The oracles are by turns whimsical, campy, jaded, or merely astute, but always provocative. They come with an attitude and all are distilled from the best stuff in sight, purged only of the most rank and incontinent sexist bile.

Plainly there is something here to offend everyone. And if this conflicted collage survives in print, its readers will look back in wonder at what manner of crisis this was. They will say that all of us—men and women, hunters and gatherers alike—were deserving fodder for stand-up comics and tabloid pundits. They will see that, stuck as we were in transitional times and caught in endless cycles of lessons learned too late, we learned that the mating game is a game, all right—a mind game like chess, with the outcome too often a stalemate. They will see that we learned, if anything, that the distinctions make a difference precisely because they complicate, amuse, exasperate, delight, oppress, and, sometimes, enlighten us. We learned, as they will, that men and women have a fragile hold on distinctions both precious and impossible—a splendid agony.

Boston
February 1996

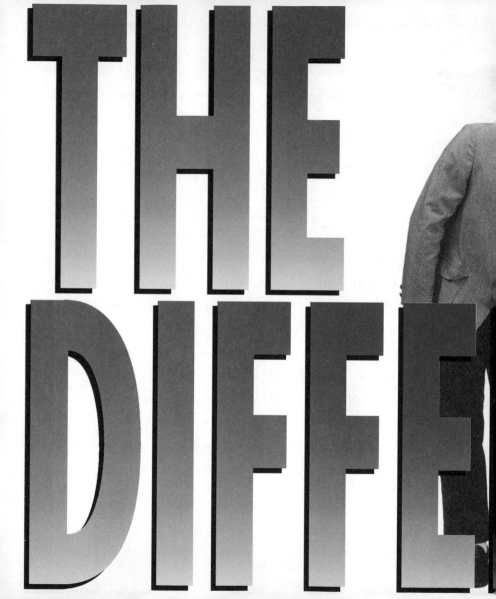

THE
DIFFE

The essential difference between men and women is that men think the Three Stooges are funny, and women don't.

Jay Leno (b. 1950)
American comedian and talk show host

The basic discovery about any people is the discovery of the relationship between its men and women.

Pearl S. Buck (1892–1973)
American writer

Men live in black and white. Women live in color.

Anonymous

Where men tell jokes, women tell stories.

Regina Barreca (b. 1957)
American scholar and writer

Women have a favorite room, men a favorite chair.

Bern Williams (b. 1929)
American writer

More and more, it appears that, biologically, men are designed for short, brutal lives and women for long miserable ones.

Estell Ramey

Women tend to see their lives as a series of chapters; men, as an arc with a clear trajectory.

Sarah Crichton

Women have a less accurate measure of time than men. There is a clock in Adam: none in Eve.

Ralph Waldo Emerson (1803–1882)
American writer and poet

Male and female are really two cultures and their life experiences are utterly different.

Kate Millet (b. 1934)
American feminist

13

We should regard loveliness as the attribute of woman,
and dignity as the attribute of man.

Cicero (106–43 B.C.)
Roman orator, statesman, and philosopher

MEN ARE WOMEN'S PLAYTHINGS; WOMAN IS THE DEVIL'S.

Victor Hugo (1802–1885)
French playwright

When novelist Margaret Atwood asked women what they feared most
from men, they said, "We're afraid they'll kill us."
When men were asked the same question about women,
they said, "We're afraid they'll laugh at us."

Naomi Wolf (b. 1962)
American writer and feminist

A man would create another man if one did not already exist, but a woman might live an eternity without even thinking of reproducing her own sex.

Johann Wolfgang von Goethe (1749–1832)
German poet and writer

Men commit actions; women commit gestures.

Phyllis Chesler (b. 1940)
American psychologist and writer

There aren't any hard women, only soft men.

Raquel Welch (b. 1942)
American actress

It is a known fact that men are practical, hardheaded realists, in contrast to women, who are romantic dreamers and actually believe that estrogenic skin cream must do something or they couldn't charge sixteen dollars for that little tiny jar.

Jane Goodsell (1921–1988)
American writer

Men prefer brief praise, pitched high; women are satisfied with praise in a lower key, just so it goes on and on.

Mignon McLaughlin
20th-century American writer and editor

What is most beautiful in virile men is something feminine;
what is most beautiful in a feminine woman is something masculine.

Susan Sontag (b. 1933)
American writer

Men are more interesting than women,
but women are more fascinating.

James Thurber (1894–1961)
American writer and humorist

If a man makes a stupid mistake, the other men say
"What a fool that man is." If a woman makes a stupid mistake,
the men say "What fools women are."

H. C. L. Jackson (1894–1954)
American writer

WOMEN ARE CURSED, AND MEN ARE THE PROOF.

Roseanne (b. 1953)
American actress and comedienne

One great difference between men and women
is that women at least know they are oppressed.

Herb Goldberg (b. 1937)
American writer

When men are oppressed, it's tragedy.
When women are oppressed, it's tradition.

Bernadette Mosala

. . . a woman's cold and a man's cold are not the same thing.
A woman's cold is a cheap excuse to get out of sex. A man
gets a cold and it's the end of the world.

Margo Kaufman (b. 1939)
Hollywood correspondent

Men resent women because women bear kids, and seem to have
this magic link with immortality that men lack. (But they should stay
home for a day with a kid; they'd change their minds.)

Tuesday Weld (b. 1943)
American actress

A woman, I have heard, takes to herself a mate and reproduces her kind, and is thereby complete; with a woman completion, I believe, signifies multiplication. As to a man, I doubt if even multiplication completes him; possibly nothing completes him; possibly he remains an imperfect creature to the end.

Rose Macaulay (1881–1958)
English writer

All men hate all women some of the time; some men hate all women all of the time; some men hate some women all of the time. Unfortunately, women cannot bring themselves to hate men, possibly because they carry them in their wombs from time to time.

Germaine Greer (b. 1939)
English writer and feminist

Men fear and hate women more than women fear and hate men. I think it is this rather than the male's superior strength that makes it possible for our civilization to be called "a man's world." It is not a contest of strength; it is a contest of hate.

Karl Menninger (1893–1990)
American psychiatrist

Women, it is true, make human beings, but only men can make men.

Margaret Mead (1901–1978)
American anthropologist

All women become like their mothers. That is their tragedy. No man does. That's his.

Oscar Wilde (1854–1900)
Irish poet and playwright

Women love hotels; men hate them.

George Bernard Shaw (1856–1950)
English playwright and critic

A man is an irrational creature who is always looking
for a home atmosphere in a hotel and hotel service at home.

Anonymous

Men *can* clean, of course, but women *do* clean.

Mary Lowndes (1868–1947)
English writer

Men make wounds and women bind them.

Nellie McClung (1873–1951)
Canadian writer and feminist

When a woman is very, very bad, she is awful,
but when a man is correspondingly good, he is weird.

Minna Antrim (1861–1950)
American writer

Women decide the questions of life correctly and quickly, not because they are lucky guessers, not because they are divinely inspired, not because they practice a magic inherited from savagery, but simply and solely because they have sense. They see at a glance what most men could not see with searchlights and telescopes; they are at grips with the essentials of a problem before men have finished debating its mere externals.

H. L. Mencken (1880–1956)
American writer and editor

Men are brought up to command, women to seduce.

Sally Kempton (b. 1943)
American writer

While women are socialized to get male attention
by being "good girls" or not offending male egos, men are
being socialized to get female attention by standing out.

Warren Farrell (b. 1943)
American psychologist and writer

A man likes you for what he thinks you are; a woman, for what you think she is.

Ivan Panin (1855–1942)
American writer

If men were as unselfish as women,
women would very soon become more selfish than men.

J. Churchton Collins (1848–1908)
English writer

A woman means by unselfishness chiefly taking trouble for others; a man means not giving trouble to others. Thus each sex regards the other as radically selfish.

C. S. Lewis (1898–1963)
English writer

Show me a woman who doesn't feel guilty and I'll show you a man.

Erica Jong (b. 1943)
American writer and poet

The man's desire is for the woman; but the woman's desire
is rarely other than for the desire of the man.

Samuel Taylor Coleridge (1772–1834)
English poet and critic

Men are more conventional than women and much slower to change their ideas.

Kathleen Norris (1880–1966)
American writer

Women are not afraid to explore their inner lives.
Men don't want to know they have one.

Ron Bass

Time and circumstance, which enlarge the views of most men,
narrow the views of women almost invariably.

Thomas Hardy (1840–1928)
English writer

The women are more emotional than men;
men are emotionally weaker than women; that is, men break
more easily under emotional strain than women do.

Ashley Montagu (b. 1905)
English-born American anthropologist

Women are as old as they feel—and men are old when they lose their feelings.

Mae West (1892–1980)
American actress

The way to a man's heart is through his stomach.
The way to a woman's heart is through the doors of a restaurant.

Lisa Cofield

THE FASTEST WAY TO A MAN'S HEART IS THROUGH HIS CHEST.

Roseanne (b. 1953)
American actress and comedienne

"Women do have hobbies. It just doesn't seem that way to men." Men do things—play football, sail boats, watch TV—to distract themselves from what's going on in their lives. Women, however, opt for activities that make their lives more bearable. Having coffee with a friend, chatting on the phone, doing yoga are her equivalent of you spending Sunday fishing.

Gael Lindenfield
English psychotherapist

Women save things from their childhood, men don't.

Rita Rudner (b. 1956)
American comedienne and actress

Contrary to general opinion, women are not as sentimental as men, but are much more hardheaded.

Taylor Caldwell (1900–1985)
English writer

Men argue for the right to be free while women argue for the right to be upset. Men want space while women want understanding.

John Gray
20th-century American writer

Man's conclusions are reached by toil.
Woman arrives at the same by sympathy.

Ralph Waldo Emerson (1803–1882)
American writer and poet

Man has his will, but woman has her way.

Oliver Wendell Holmes (1809–1894)
American physician, poet, essayist, and writer

Man is kind only to be cruel; woman cruel only to be kind.

Minna Antrim (1861–1950)
American writer

The weakness of men is the facade of strength; the strength of women is the facade of strength.

Lawrence Diggs (b. 1947)
American politician

It is fatal to be a man or woman pure and simple:
one must be a woman manly, or a man womanly.

Virginia Woolf (1882–1941)
English writer and critic

Have you ever noticed that what passes as a terrific man
would only be an adequate woman?

Anna Quindlen (b. 1953)
American writer

A woman's guess is much more accurate than a man's certainty.

Rudyard Kipling (1865–1936)
English writer and poet

Most men aren't so handsome that they can afford to play fast and loose with the little the good Lord gave them. I suppose when He took one look at Adam and realized what He'd done, He simply had to give women loving hearts to overcome the handicap.

Matilda Stevens

The great truth is that women actually like men,
and men can never believe it.

Isabel Patterson

Women grow attached to men through the favors they grant them;
but men, through the same favors, are cured of their love.

Jean de La Bruyère (1645–1696)
French philosopher and writer

Women cannot help moving, and men cannot help being moved.

Anthony Burgess (1917–1993)
English writer

The woman possesses a theatrical exterior and a circumspect interior, while in the man it is the interior which is theatrical. The woman goes to the theater; the man carries it inside himself and is the impresario of his own life.

Jose Ortega y Gasset (1883–1955)
Spanish writer and philosopher

Women are nine times more talkative than men.

Anonymous

Women eat while they talk, men talk while they eat. At table, men talk for a long time between mouthfuls, women while eating.

Malcolm de Chazal (b. 1902)
French writer

Women tend to qualify more than men. They put "perhaps" and "I think" and use diminutives more than men.

Gail Godwin (b. 1937)
American writer

Women on average will speak 7,000 words in a day; men, 2,000. That explains a lot . . . So many times I come home, my wife swears to me I'm in a bad mood or I'm mad at her. Now I realize, I'm just out of words. I've already done my 2,000. She's got 5,000 left.

Rob Becker (b. 1958)
American comedian

Women prefer to talk in twos, while men prefer to talk in threes.

G. K. Chesterton (1874–1936)
English writer

I am struck by the observation—which has not changed in 17 years—that two women are roughly ten times more likely to be talking about the problems with the men in their lives as are two men to be discussing their problems with women.

Warren Farrell (b. 1943)
American psychologist and writer

Women deprived of the company of men pine, men deprived of the company of women become stupid.

Anton Chekhov (1860–1904)
Russian playwright and writer

Women have more imagination than men.
They need it to tell us how wonderful we are.

Arnold H. Glasow

A wise woman puts a grain of sugar into everything she says to a man, and takes a grain of salt with everything he says to her.

Helen Rowland (1875–1950)
American writer

A good cigar is as great a comfort to a man as a good cry is to a woman.

Edward Bulwer-Lytton (1831–1891)
English statesman

Men, not women, hang up the telephone receiver. Women always believe that there is happiness at the other end of the line.

Henry Millon de Montherlant (1896–1972)
French writer

Women never know when the curtain has fallen.
They always want a sixth act, and as soon as the interest
in the play is entirely over, they propose to continue it.

Oscar Wilde (1854–1900)
Irish poet and playwright

Men want to put their signature at the bottom;
women don't want to finish that letter.

Ian Shoales [Merle Kessler] (b. 1949)
American writer

If women are often frustrated because men do not respond
to their troubles by offering matching troubles,
men are often frustrated because women do.

Deborah Tannen (b. 1945)
American linguist and writer

Women have their faults. Men have only two.
Everything they say. Everything they do.

Anonymous

Women like silent men. They think they're listening.

Marcel Achard (1899–1974)
French playwright and director

The most frequently expressed complaint women have about men is that men don't listen. The most frequently expressed complaint men have about women is that women are always trying to change them.

John Gray
20th-century American writer

There is no woman Mozart because
there is no woman Jack the Ripper.
Men are more prone to obsession because
they are fleeing domination by women.

Camille Paglia (b. 1946)
American writer

There is no such thing as a dangerous woman; there are only susceptible men.

Joseph Wood Krutch (1893–1970)
American writer and critic

If you would understand men, study women.

French proverb

Women know about life and about how to get along with others, and are sensitive to beauty, and can yell louder. They know all about guys, having been exposed to guy life since forever, and guys know nothing about girls except that they want one desperately. Which gender is better equipped to manipulate the other?

Garrison Keillor (b. 1942)
American writer and radio host

What Women want: to be loved, listened to, desired, respected, needed, and trusted
What Men want: Tickets for the World Series.

Feminist T-shirt slogan

Some differences are very pronounced and quite unexpected. For example, men are less sensitive to extreme heat and more sensitive to extreme cold. Men have better daylight vision; women have better night vision . . . men have faster reaction times and are more interested in objects than people. Men are better at spatial thinking than women are. For example, they can mentally rotate an object easier than women can . . . Women hear better, especially at the higher ranges.

Robert Wallace (b. 1919)
American writer

The main difference between men and women is that men are lunatics and women are idiots.

Rebecca West (1892–1983)
Irish writer

Most women have all other women as adversaries;
most men have all other men as their allies.

Gelett Burgess (1866–1951)
American writer

A man needs a witness to his masculinity. He needs other men to see how well he's doing. A woman gets her femininity boosted if she has the undivided attention of one man. Having several men present doesn't increase the effect, it simply dilutes it.

Gael Lindenfield
English psychotherapist

A man strikes a match toward himself, a woman away.

from *Esquire*

Men get that remote control in their hands, they don't even know what the hell they're not watching. You know we just keep going . . . Women will stop and go, "Well, let me see what the show is before I change the channel" . . . Because women nest and men hunt. That's why we watch TV differently.

Jerry Seinfeld (b. 1954)
American actor and comedian

Of the people who send in their life list to the American Birding Association, about 90 percent are male. I guess it's because the collecting, the drivenness, the hunting instinct tends to be male, whereas women are more automatically drawn to the beauty and flight and freedom of birds and then only secondarily do they amass their list.

John Leo
20th-century American journalist

THE '90S SEEM TO HAVE PRODUCED TWO SEXES—WOMEN AND ASSHOLES.

Rob Becker (b. 1958)
American comedian

On how women and men pay for cabs when there are two or three women together as opposed to two or three men: "With men, each guy volunteers to pay the full amount; with the ladies, they divide the fare by two or three—right down to the penny; and then, as an afterthought, remember the tip, debate about what they usually give for a tip, and then divide that—also to the penny."

New York City cab driver

How men hate waiting while their wives shop for clothes and trinkets; how woman hate waiting, often for much of their lives, while their husbands shop for fame and glory.

Thomas Szasz (b. 1920)
Hungarian-born American psychiatrist and writer

Men are foolish: they think money should be taken from the rich and given to the poor. Women are sensible: they think money should be taken from the rich and given to them.

Richard J. Needham (b. 1912)
Canadian writer

Men play the game; women know the score.

Roger Woddis
English poet

A successful man is one who makes more money than his wife can spend. A successful women is one who can find such a man.

Lana Turner (1920–1995)
American actress

Men writers aren't thought of as "men writers," they are thought of as great writers! It would be fine if they would be called "men writers." It just never comes up—"Updike or Bellow, he's a really great man writer." But we frequently hear "Margaret Atwood is a really incredible woman writer." I say what a crock of shit.

Anne Lamott (b. 1954)
American writer

Men see objects, women see the relationship between objects. Whether the objects need each other, love each other, match each other. It is an extra dimension of feeling we men are without and one that makes war abhorrent to all real women—and absurd.

Michel Foucault (1926–1984)
French philosopher

Women make much better soldiers than men.
They always know where the real enemy is hidden.

Jose Yglesias
20th-century American writer

Women who are living in battle zones turn solitary and introspective, completely repulsed by the idea of coupling, while men basically find war to be a big turn-on, the ultimate aftershave.

Kathy McManus (b. 1948)
American writer

I'm not denyin' the women are foolish: God Almighty made 'em to match the men.

George Eliot [Mary Ann Evans] (1819–1880)
English writer

The men who espoused unpopular causes may have been considered misguided, but they were rarely attacked for their morals or their masculinity. Women who did the same thing were apt to be denounced as harlots or condemned for being unfeminine—an all-purpose word that was used to describe almost any category of female behavior of which men disapproved.

Margaret Truman (b. 1924)
American writer

Women are more irritable than men, probably because men are more irritating.

Anonymous

Men are made to be managed, and women are born managers.

George Meredith (1828–1909)
English writer and poet

The silliest woman can manage a clever man;
but it needs a really clever woman to manage a fool.

Rudyard Kipling (1865–1936)
English writer and poet

Anyone who believes that men and women have the same mindset
hasn't lived on earth. A man thinks that everything
he does is wonderful. A woman has doubts.

Margo Kaufman (b. 1939)
Hollywood correspondent

Men are irrelevant. Women are happy or unhappy,
fulfilled or unfulfilled, and it has nothing to do with men.

Fay Weldon

Male energy tends to scatter and destroy, female to gather and construct.

Charlotte Perkins Gilman (1860–1935)
American writer and feminist

A man thinks he knows, but a woman knows better.

Chinese proverb

The ability to have our own way, and at the same time convince others they are having their own way, is a rare thing among men. Among women it is as common as eyebrows.

Thomas Baily Aldrich (1836–1907)
American writer

Verily, men do foolish things thoughtlessly, knowing not why; but no woman doeth aught without a reason.

Gelett Burgess (1866–1951)
American writer

There are two sides to the story when men quarrel, but at least a dozen when women quarrel.

Edgar Watson Howe (1853–1937)
American writer

A woman need know only one man well, in order to understand all men; whereas a man may know all women and understand not one of them.

Helen Rowland (1875–1950)
American writer

With a woman first thoughts are best, with a man, second thoughts.

Italian proverb

Men live by forgetting—women live on memories.

T. S. Eliot (1888–1965)
American writer

A man keeps another's secrets better than he does his own.
A woman, on the other hand, keeps her own better than another's.

Jean de La Bruyère (1645–1696)
French philosopher and writer

In men, the mind is connected to the brain.
In women, the mind is connected to the heart.

Amy Tan (b. 1952)
American writer

Men want to feel competent and appreciated, but sometimes have to be alone; women need to feel loved and to share their feelings.

Jerry Adler

Men are virtuous because the women are;
women are virtuous from necessity.

Edgar Watson Howe (1853–1937)
American writer

Men choose the self and women choose others.

Mary Field Belenky

God made men stronger, but not necessarily more intelligent. He gave women intuition and femininity. And, used properly, that combination easily jumbles the brain of any man I've ever met.

Farrah Fawcett (b. 1947)
American actress

Women are quite unlike men. Women have higher voices, longer hair, smaller waistlines, daintier feet and prettier hands. They also invariably have the upper hand.

Stephen Potter (1900–1969)
English writer

Men, the very best of men, can only suffer, while women can endure.

Dinah Mulock Craik (1826–1887)
English writer

Women find their inspiration in the stress of moments
that for men are merely awful, absurd or futile.

Joseph Conrad (1857–1924)
English writer

I think the real difference between men and women is their way of suffering. A woman learns to accept suffering, in body and spirit. But a man keeps struggling, and the struggle keeps weakening and finally defeats him. Suffering never weakens or defeats a woman. It becomes a part of her. It brings her closer to life. With a man it's different. It brings him closer to death.

Frederic Prokosch (1908–1989)
American writer

Destiny is something men select; women achieve it
only by default or stupendous suffering.

Harriet Rosenstein

A man has only one aim in life.
A woman has three, all contradictory.

Benoite Groult (b. 1920)
French writer

Man weeps to think that he will die so soon; woman, that she was born so long ago.

H. L. Mencken (1880–1956)
American writer and editor

Men mourn for what they have lost;
women for what they ain't got.

Josh Billings [Henry Wheller Shaw] (1818–1889)
American writer

A woman is a woman until the day she dies, but a man's a man only as long as he can.

Jackie "Moms" Mabley (1894–1975)
American singer and comedienne

When women write about dying, there is always a graceful resignation in the line, a tone of "Ah, it's here," riding somewhere between fatalism and an embrace. When a man writes about dying, he assails the fact with an in-your-face.

Roger Rosenblatt (b. 1940)
American writer

Men use their heads. Women use their emotions.

from *Honeymoon in Bali*

Men are motivated and empowered when they feel needed. Women are motivated and empowered when they feel cherished.

John Gray
20th-century American writer

Why are women wearing perfumes that smell like flowers? Men don't like flowers. I've been wearing a great scent. It's called New Car Interior.

Rita Rudner (b. 1956)
American comedienne and actress

When it comes to buying cars, men are the emotional ones, while women are rational.

Anemona Hartocollis

A woman is incapable of feeling love for an automobile.

Bernard De Voto (1897–1955)
American writer

Several men I can think of are as capable, as smart, as funny, as compassionate, and as confused—as remarkable, you might say—as most women.

Jane Howard (b. 1935)
American writer

ONE THING IN WHICH THE SEXES ARE EQUAL IS IN THINKING THAT THEY'RE NOT.

Franklin P. Jones (b. 1906)
Writer

STYLE

Women are never disarmed by compliments. Men always are.
That is the difference between the sexes.

Oscar Wilde (1854–1900)
Irish poet and playwright

A man is as old as he feels. A woman is as old as she looks.

American saying

A WOMAN IS AS OLD AS SHE LOOKS.
A MAN IS OLD WHEN HE STOPS LOOKING.

B. C. Preston

Men come of age at sixty, women at fifteen.

James Stephens (1892–1971)
American writer

Women age, but men mature.

Gloria Steinem (b. 1934)
American writer and feminist

Women, as they grow older, rely more and more on cosmetics.
Men, as they grow older, rely more and more upon a sense of humor.

George Jean Nathan (1882–1958)
American editor and critic

Wrinkles on men is character; on women, it's "Oh, shit!" You can be Hugh Hefner at sixty and have a baby with a twenty-one-year-old and it's not seen as vampiric. But if a woman does it, it's pathetic.

Carrie Fisher (b. 1956)
American actress and writer

MEN WAKE UP AS GOOD-LOOKING AS THEY WENT TO BED. WOMEN SOMEHOW DETERIORATE DURING THE NIGHT.

Elayne Boosler (b. 1952)
American comedienne

Men can be made attractive by scars that would ruin a woman.

Irma Kurtz (b. 1935)
American writer

WOMEN ALWAYS THINK THEIR REAR ENDS ARE TOO BIG. . . THERE'S NOTHING YOU CAN SAY ABOUT A WOMAN'S BUTT THAT DOESN'T MAKE HER SUSPICIOUS. THERE ARE MANY THEORIES WHY, BUT I'M CERTAIN IT'S BECAUSE THE DERRIERE IS A WOMAN'S WEAKEST AREA. SHE CAN'T POWDER IT. SHE CAN'T USE CONCEALER. IT'S ACTUALLY TOO FAR AWAY TO REACH. IT'S SOMETHING THEY CAN'T CONTROL, AND THEY LIKE CONTROLLING EVERYTHING THAT HAS ANYTHING TO DO WITH THEIR APPEARANCE.—TIM ALLEN (B. 1953) AMERICAN ACTOR AND COMEDIAN

Men are allowed to be bald and fat and ugly and still deliver the news.
There are no bald, fat and ugly women delivering the news.

Connie Chung (b. 1946)
American broadcast journalist

YOU GUYS, YOU GAIN THIRTY POUNDS AND WE CALL YOU CUDDLY. WE GAIN AN OUNCE AND YOU CALL US TAXIS. THEN YOU DON'T CALL US AT ALL.

Carol Siskind

While women unrealistically distort their bodies negatively,
men unrealistically distort theirs positively.

Naomi Wolf (b. 1962)
American writer and feminist

There is a fascinating difference between the way men and women see themselves in a mirror. A man . . . sees Mr. America, not a ghastly, ungroomed creature . . . Women are inclined to see their flaws rather than their assets. A woman looks in the mirror and thinks "I need more lipstick" or "I look tired today." Even the most beautiful women.

Joyce Brothers (b. 1928)
American television personality and psychologist

Being a sex symbol has to do with an attitude, not looks.
Most men think it's looks, most women know otherwise.

Kathleen Turner (b. 1954)
American actress

Men look at themselves in mirrors. Women look for themselves.

Elissa Melamed

Men have an easier time buying bathing suits.
Women have two types: depressing and more depressing.
Men have two types: nerdy and not nerdy.

Rita Rudner (b. 1956)
American comedienne and actress

Men will make all sorts of allowances for a pretty woman, and a woman for an unmarried man.

Mignon McLaughlin
20th-century American writer and editor

When a man gets up to speak, people listen, then look. When a woman
gets up, people look; then, if they like what they see, they listen.

Pauline Frederick (1883–1938)
American actress

*Remember, Ginger Rogers did everything Fred Astaire did,
but she did it backwards and in high heels.*

Faith Whittlesey

A woman can look both moral and exciting—if she also looks
as if it was quite a struggle.

Edna Ferber (1887–1968)
American writer

Plain women know more about men than beautiful ones do.

Katharine Hepburn (b. 1909)
American actress

THERE ARE NO UGLY WOMEN, ONLY LAZY ONES.

Helena Rubenstein (1870–1965)
American cosmetics executive

I live by a man's code, designed to fit a man's world,
yet at the same time I never forget that a woman's first job
is to choose the right shade of lipstick.

Carole Lombard (1908–1942)
American actress

A spectacle that depresses the male and makes him shudder is that of a woman looking another woman up and down to see what she is wearing. The cold, flat look that comes into a woman's eyes when she does this, the swift coarsening of her countenance and the immediate evaporation from it of all humane quality, is one reason why men fear women.

James Thurber (1894–1961)
American writer and humorist

Women dress alike all over the world:
they dress to be annoying to other women.

Elsa Schiaparelli (1890–1973)
Italian fashion designer

I always thought the difference between men and women was pockets.

Susan Stamberg (b. 1938)
American broadcaster and writer

Men are obsessed with cleavage, women are obsessed with shoes.

Jerry Seinfeld (b. 1954)
American actor and comedian

The difference between men and women is that a man can walk past a shoe store, especially if he already has a pair of shoes.

Gallagher
20th-century American comedian

Men's clothes are so much more comfortable than women's. Take their shoes. They've got room for five toes—in each shoe.

Betsy Salkind

A man inspects the sole of his shoe by crooking his leg in front. A woman slips her foot behind her and looks over her shoulder.

from *Esquire*

I much prefer being a man. Women have to spend so much time pulling themselves together, and their shoes kill their feet. I know. And they don't have the freedom that men do. I can walk into this place and that place, and go anywhere I want to, where women can't.

Lynne Carter
20th-century Female impersonator

Women are born to shop . . . Men are born to invest,
and are then evasive and deceitful about their losses and gains.

Asa Baber (b. 1936)
American writer and editor

When women are depressed they either eat or go shopping.
Men invade another country. It's a whole different way of thinking.

Elayne Boosler (b. 1952)
American comedienne

A man is a person who will pay two dollars for a one-dollar item he wants.
A woman will pay one dollar for a two-dollar item she doesn't want.

William Binger

A woman will buy anything she thinks a store is losing money on.

Frank "Kin" McKinney Hubbard (1868–1930)
American journalist

A new hat has the same effect upon a woman
that three cocktails have upon a man.

Jay E. House (1870–1936)
Writer

Why is it that when a man's clothes don't fit it's the clothes' fault, and when the woman's clothes don't fit it's the woman's fault?

Karen De Witt

Another difference between the sexes is that a woman's slip always pulls down while a man's shirt always creeps up.

Anonymous

Men have better self-images than women.
You know what I've never seen in a men's magazine? A makeover.

Rita Rudner (b. 1956)
American comedienne and actress

Women wearing men's clothes are chic; men wearing women's clothes make us fall on the floor laughing.

Cynthia Heimel (b. 1947)
American writer and playwright

Women aren't embarrassed when they buy men's pajamas, but a man buying a nightgown acts as though he were dealing with a dope peddler.

Jimmy Cannon (1909–1973)
American journalist

In our civilization, men are afraid that they will not be men enough
and women are afraid that they might be considered only women.

Theodor Reik (1888–1969)
Psychologist and writer

**Women constitute half the world's population, perform nearly two-thirds
of its work hours, receive one-tenth of the world's income and
own less than one hundredth of the world's property.**

United Nations Report, 1980

Women are the only exploited group in history
who have been idealized into powerlessness.

Francine du Plessix Gray

Power for men means the ability to make things happen . . .
The female definition of power is the ability not to have to please.

Lois Gould (b. 1938) and Susan Stamberg (b. 1938)
American broadcasters and writers

The woman's position in the world today is so much harder than a man's that it makes me choke every time I hear a man complain about *anything!*

Katharine Hepburn (b. 1909)
American actress

If you want anything said, ask a man.
If you want anything done, ask a woman.

Margaret Thatcher (b. 1925)
British prime minister

Men are cleverer than women at reasoning, women are cleverer than men at drawing conclusions. A parliament in which the members were predominantly women would get through its legislation much faster.

Malcolm de Chazal (b. 1902)
French writer

Happiness isn't so bad for a woman . . . she gets fatter, she gets older, she could lie down, nuzzling a regimen of men and little kids, she could just die of pleasure. But men are different, they have to own money, or they have to be famous, or everybody on the block has to look up to them from the cellar stairs. A woman counts her children, and acts snotty, like she invented life, but men must do well in the world. I know that men are not fooled by being happy.

Grace Paley (b. 1922)
American writer

Men always want to please women, but these past 15 years, women have been hard to please. If you want to resist the feminist movement, the simple way to do it is to give them what they want and they'll defeat themselves. Today, there are women in their 20s and 30s who don't know if they want to be a mother, have lunch, or be secretary of state.

Jack Nicholson (b. 1937)
American actor

Women's liberation is just a lot of foolishness. It's the men who are discriminated against. They can't bear children. And no one's likely to do anything about that.

Golda Meir (1898–1978)
Israeli prime minister

I'm furious about the women's liberationists. They keep getting up on soapboxes and proclaiming women are brighter than men. That's true, but it should be kept quiet or it ruins the whole racket.

Anita Loos (1893–1981)
American writer and playwright

Women are being considered as candidates for Vice President of the United States because it is the worst job in America. It's amazing that men will take it. A job with real power is First Lady. I'd be willing to run for that. As far as the men who are running for President are concerned, they aren't even people I would date.

Nora Ephron (b. 1941)
American writer and screenwriter

Women who insist upon having the same options as men would do well to consider the option of being the strong silent type.

Fran Lebowitz (b. 1950)
American writer

Women don't get hung up making deals the way men do.

Shirley Chisholm (b. 1924)
American politician and writer

Real equality is going to come not when a female Einstein is recognized as quickly as a male Einstein, but when a female schlemiel is promoted as quickly as a male schlemiel.

Bella Abzug (b. 1920)
American lawyer and politician

There are very few jobs that actually require a penis or a vagina. All other jobs should be open to everybody.

Florence Kennedy (b. 1916)
American lawyer

If a man fights his adversaries, he's called determined.
If a woman does, she's frustrated.

Esther Peterson (b. 1934)
American writer

Men work to achieve goals. Women work to prevent catastrophe.

quoted by Penney Kome

The world would be a far better place if more men wanted to become women, than women wanted to become men.

Albert Halsey (b. 1923)
English professor, editor, and writer

Men fear and hate women more than women fear and hate men. I think is this rather than the male's superior strength that makes it possible for our civilization to be called "a man's world." It is not a contest of strength; it is a contest of hate.

Karl Menninger (1893–1990)
American psychiatrist

Whatever women do they must do twice as well as men to be thought half has good. Luckily, this is not difficult.

Charlotte Whitton (1896–1975)
Canadian politician and writer

Once a woman is made man's equal, she becomes his superior.

Margaret Thatcher (b. 1925)
British prime minister

Women in general want to be loved for what they are and men for what they accomplish.

Theodor Reik (1888–1969)
Psychologist and writer

Men readily interrupt the speech of women, and women allow the interruption.

Susan Brownmiller (b. 1935)
American writer

A man at his desk in a room with a closed door is a man at work.
A woman at her desk in any room is available.

Betty Rollin (b. 1936)
Writer

A man has to be Joe McCarthy to be called ruthless.
All a woman has to do is put you on hold.

Marlo Thomas (b. 1943)
American actress

"Why the hell don't women ever make a scene? Men are always making scenes, yelling in the halls. Why can't you yell in the halls?"

"Because," she sighed, "women don't get away with yelling in the halls. They call you a hysterical bitch if you yell in the halls."

"Also," Sophy noted wryly, "they fire you. It's *their* halls."

Lois Gold (b. 1945)
American writer

When a man gives his opinion, he's a man.
When a woman gives her opinion, she's a bitch.

Bette Davis (1908–1989)
American actress

If a man mulls over a decision, they say "He's weighing his options."
If a woman does it, they say "She can't make up her mind."

Barbara Proctor
Writer

A man may brave opinion; a woman must submit to it.

Germaine de Stael (1766–1817)
French writer

Men are taught to apologize for their weaknesses,
women for their strengths.

Lois Wyse (b. 1951)
American writer

A man is as good as he has to be, and a woman is as bad as she dares.

Elbert Hubbard (1856–1915)
American writer and editor

Every man who is high up likes to feel that he has done it himself;
and the wife smiles, and lets it go at that. It's our only joke. Every
woman knows that.

James M. Barrie (1860–1937)
Scottish writer

Relatio

The two sexes mutually corrupt and improve each other.

Mary Wollstonecraft (1759–1797)
English writer

Diamonds are a girl's best friend. Dogs are a man's best friend. Now you know which sex is smarter.

Anonymous

A man criticizes his enemies behind their backs; a woman, her friends.

Anonymous

Women joke that "If you're really a friend, you're on my speed dial." With men, it's more like "If I'm really your friend, you have a nickname for me."

Ira Bachrach

. . . best friends who haven't seen each other in a while, gal version: "You're my oldest and closest friend." Best friends who haven't seen each other in a while, guy version: "Still driving that piece of shit?" They mean exactly the same thing.

Rob Becker (b. 1958)
American comedian

In social interactions, two women talking together look into each other's eyes far more often than two men would do.

Dianne Hales

Men friends are shoulder to shoulder.
Female friends are more often eye to eye.

Louise Bernikow (b. 1940)
American writer

Friendship has too much resembled for men the camaraderie of battle, for women the consolations of passivity.

Carolyn G. Heilbrun (b. 1926)
American writer

By and large men do prefer the company of other men, not only in their structured time but in the time they fill with optional, nonobligatory activity. They prefer to play games, drink and talk, as well as work and fight together. Yet something is missing. Despite the time men spend together, their contact rarely goes beyond the external, a limitation which tends to make their friendships shallow and unsatisfying.

Marc Feigen Fasteau (b. 1942)
American writer

After an acquaintance of ten minutes many women will exchange confidences that a man would not reveal to a lifelong friend.

Page Smith (b. 1917)
American historian

Men kick friendship around like a football, but it doesn't seem to crack.
Women treat it like glass and it goes to pieces.

Anne Morrow Lindbergh (b. 1907)
American writer and aviator

The difference between men friends and women friends
is that men tend to do things together, women tend just to be together.

Art Jahnke

For a man, a woman can be either a vessel or a friend; for a woman,
unless a man is her friend, sex is a merely a temporary connection.

Alice Koller

HARRY: No man can be friends with a woman he finds attractive. He always wants to have sex with her.

SALLY: So you're saying a man can be friends with a woman he finds unattractive.

HARRY: No, you pretty much want to nail them, too.

from *When Harry Met Sally*

Those who always speak well of women do not know them sufficiently; those who always speak ill of them do not know them at all.

Guillaume Pigault Lebrun

Why is a woman persistently regarded as a mystery?
It is not that she has labored to conceal the organic
and psychological facts of her constitution, but that men
have showed no interest in exploring them.

Ruth Hershberger

One of the most persistent myths of love is that a man, once he is taken with a woman, is ensnared by her indifference toward him. The truth is that, while such indifference may keep him stepping lively for a short time, it soon causes him to get out of the race altogether.

The clever woman realizes that the best way to get her man is to throw away all traditional weapons and frankly and openly tell him that she likes him. The man thus handled, all folklore to the contrary, is won.

George Jean Nathan (1882–1958)
American editor and critic

It is not true that men prefer foolish women. Rather they prefer women who can simulate foolishness whenever necessary, which is the very core of intelligence.

Paul Eldridge
20th-century American writer

He took my glasses off and said, "Without your glasses, why, you're beautiful." I said, "Without my glasses, you're not half bad either."

Kit Hollerbach

A woman who takes things from a man is called a girlfriend.
A man who takes things from a woman is called a gigolo.

Ruthie Stein

The main result of feminism has been the Dutch Treat.

Nora Ephron (b. 1941)
American writer and screenwriter

Men, and only men, play the air guitar. In his heart, a man thinks it's cool when he's plucking his magical, musical air guitar. In her heart, a woman knows her date looks like a dork.

Sandra L. Beckwith

Men are like St. Bernards. Women love the fact that we lick their faces, but they hate the saliva. They love cuddling us, but they hate taking us for a walk. We shed, we need some exercise . . . and we knock stuff over. That's the deal. Give us a break.

from *Hot and Bothered*

You know, it's women like you who make men like me
make women like you make men like me.

from *The Iceman's Ball*

Eloquence might get you started with a woman
but it is often taciturnity that seals the bargain.

Clive James (b. 1939)
American journalist

Men who have everything seem to want just one thing more. They want a woman whose heart of gold beats staunchly in a thirty-eight-inch chest.

Elizabeth Kaye

Woman's virtue is man's greatest invention.

Cornelia Otis Skinner (1901–1979)
American actress and writer

In relationships, men pull back and then get close, while women rise and fall in their ability to love themselves and others . . . Men are like rubber bands . . . A woman is like a wave.

John Gray
20th-century American writer

Once a woman has forgiven her man, she must not reheat his sins for breakfast.

Marlene Dietrich (1901–1992)
American actress and singer

Most men's primary fantasy is still, unfortunately, access to a number of beautiful women. For a man, commitment means giving up this fantasy. Most women's primary fantasy is a relationship with one man who either provides economic security or is on his way to doing so (he has "potential"). For a woman, commitment to this type of man means achieving this fantasy. So commitment often means that a woman achieves her primary fantasy, while a man gives his up.

Warren Farrell (b. 1943)
American psychologist and writer

"Men get into a new relationship before they've hardly left the old one." From the outside it looks like you've moved on. . . Women are better at feeling terrible. When a relationship breaks up they talk to their friends, their mother, they cry a lot and then, after a year or two, they meet someone else, dry their eyes, and throw themselves into the future with barely a backward glance.

Joel Mahabir
English psychotherapist

Men are shits. It hit me when I realized that I wouldn't take myself out or go to bed with me.

from *Tootsie*

Men's vows are women's traitors.

William Shakespeare (1564–1616)
English playwright and poet

Men don't understand, as a rule,
that women like to get used to them by degrees.

John Oliver Hobbes (1867–1906)
American writer

Today a woman without a man is like a fish without a bicycle.

Attributed to Gloria Steinem (b. 1934)
American writer and feminist

It's a sickness with a lot of women. Always looking for a new way to get hurt by a new man. Get smart: there hasn't been a new man since Adam.

from *House of Strangers*

I don't know why women want any of the things that men have when one of the things that women have is men.

Coco Chanel (1882–1971)
French fashion designer

You see an awful lot of smart guys with dumb women,
but you hardly ever see a smart woman with a dumb guy.

Erica Jong (b. 1942)
American writer and poet

Even the wisest men make fools of themselves about women, and even the most foolish women are wise about men.

Theodor Reik (1888–1969)
Psychologist and writer

All men, except the most brutish, desire to have, in the woman most nearly connected with them, not a forced slave but a willing one.

John Stuart Mill (1806–1873)
English philosopher and economist

My message to men is,
"Don't screw around with women
because they can turn around
and screw you back."

Jackie Collins (b. 1941)
American writer

I expect that Woman will be the last thing civilized by Man.

George Meredith (1828–1909)
English writer and poet

The man-woman thing is a boring subject. It's essentially a dead end. It's going to come down to one of two things: either you're going to take off your clothes or you're not.

Nikki Giovanni (b. 1943)
American writer and poet

The human comedy begins with a vertical smile.

Richard Condon (b. 1915)
American writer

Sex is dirty only when it's done right.

Woody Allen (b. 1935)
American actor, director, and writer

While man has a sex, woman is a sex.

Elizabeth Belfort Bax (1854–1926)
English writer

Sexual intercourse is kicking death in the ass while singing.

Charles Bukowski (1920–1994)
American writer

The first thing that strikes the careless observer is that women are unlike men. They are "the opposite sex"—though why "opposite" I do not know; what is the "neighboring sex"?

Dorothy Sayers (1893–1957)
English writer

You're not supposed to mention fucking in mixed company, and yet that's precisely the place you're supposed to do it.

George Carlin (b. 1937)
American comedian

Women are the most powerful magnet in the universe. And all men are cheap metal. And we all know where north is.

Larry Miller (b. 1943)
American broadcasting executive

A man must be potent and orgasmic to ensure the future of the race. A woman need only be available.

William H. Masters (b. 1915) American physician
and Virginia E. Johnson (b. 1925) American psychologist

Men get laid but women get screwed.

Quentin Crisp (b. 1908)
English writer

Women understand better than men how important and how insignificant sex can be. . . . Men are interested in having their sexuality in a box; women see it as the unruly beast that it is.

Sallie Tisdale (b. 1957)
American writer

If you aren't going all the way, why go at all?

Joe Namath (b. 1943)
American athlete and sportscaster

When it comes to reporting sexual activity, men and women bend the truth, in opposite directions. Men exaggerate and women understate.

from the *New York Times Magazine*

When a man falls in love, he wants to go to bed.
When a woman falls in love, she wants to talk about it.

Mignon McLaughlin
20th-century American writer and editor

Every man, whether he be young or old,
when meeting any woman, measures the potentiality of sex
between them. Thus it has always been with me.

Charlie Chaplin (1889–1977)
English comedian, actor, and director

Sex is first of all a very visual thing. A man walks through the door,
and I think, yes I would, no I wouldn't. And any woman who says
she doesn't think that way, at least for a second, is a liar.

Soraya Khashoggi (b. 1946)
Writer

When a man goes on a date
he wonders if he is going to get lucky.
A woman already knows.

Frederike Ryder

Women need a reason to have sex—men just need a place.

Billy Crystal (b. 1947)
American actor and comedian

In women sex corrects banality, in men it aggravates it.

Joaquim Maria Machado de Assis (1839–1908)
Brazilian writer

Men are like firemen. To us, sex is an emergency, and no matter what we're doing we can be ready in two minutes. Women, on the other hand, are like fire. They're very exciting, but the conditions have to be exactly right for it to occur.

Jerry Seinfeld (b. 1954)
American actor and comedian

To succeed with the opposite sex, tell her you're impotent. She can't wait to disprove it.

Cary Grant (1904–1986)
English-born American actor

Women always lie to men during sex to manipulate them: Honey, you're so big I had to order a diaphragm with an airbag.

Felicia Michaels

The real problem between the sexes is that for men, sex is a gender-underliner, they need it for their egos. We don't need sex to make us feel we are the persons we need to be.

Carol Clewlow (b. 1916)
American writer

When a woman ends an affair, she turns to her women friends. When a man ends an affair, he starts another one. Thank God.

Sydney Harris (1917–1986)
American writer

I love the lines the men use to get us into bed. "Please, I'll only put it in for a minute." What am I, a microwave?

Beverly Mickins
American comedienne

Woman is: finally screwing and your groin and buttocks and thighs ache like hell and you're all wet and maybe bloody and it wasn't like a Hollywood movie at all but Jesus at least you're not a virgin any more but is this what it's all about? And meanwhile, he's asking "Did you come?"

Robin Morgan (b. 1941)
American writer and editor

It is naive in the extreme for women to expect to be regarded as equals by men . . . so long as they persist in a subhuman (i.e. animal like) behavior during sexual intercourse. I'm referring to the outlandish panting, gasping, moaning, sobbing, writhing, scratching, biting, screaming conniptions, and the seemingly invariable "OH MY GOD . . . OH MY GOD" all so predictably integral to pre- and post-, and orgasmic stages of intercourse.

Terry Southern (b. 1924)
American writer

Men always fall for frigid women because they put on the best show.

Fannie Brice (1891–1951)
American actress and singer

The only jobs for which no man is qualified are human incubator and wet nurse. Likewise, the only job for which no woman is or can be qualified is sperm donor.

Wilma Scott Heide

One puzzling thing about men—they allow their sex instincts to drive them to where their intelligence never would take them.

Joan Fontaine (b. 1917)
American actress

Men learn to love the women they are attracted to
and women become attracted to the men they love.

from *Sex, Lies and Videotape*

Women are cynical about being used as sex objects.
Which is a shame, because it's fun to use your sexuality.

Kim Basinger (b. 1953)
American actress

There are two kinds of women: those who want power in the world
and those who want power in bed.

Jacqueline Kennedy Onassis (1929–1994)
American editor and First Lady

Man's greatest advantage in the battle of the sexes is woman's curiosity.

Louis L'Amour (1908–1988)
American writer

Dames were put on this earth to weaken us, drain our energy,
laugh at us when they see us naked.

from *Johnny Dangerously*

If men had their way a woman would lie down a prostitute and get up a virgin.

from *Enemies: A Love Story*

I dress for women—and I undress for men.

Angie Dickinson (b. 1932)
American actress

Men think they know a woman if they've seen her naked.

from *The Middle of the World*

For a woman to be loved, she usually ought to be naked.

Pierre Cardin (b. 1922)
French fashion designer

Outside every thin woman is a fat man trying to get in.

Katharine Whitehorn (b. 1928)
English writer

Do you know why God withheld the sense of humor from women?
So that we may love you instead of laughing at you.

Mrs. Patrick Campbell (1865–1940)
English actress

Women must pretend not to be willing—men must always
pretend not to be aware of the fact.

Hildric Davenport

The great discovery of the age is that women like it too.

Hugh MacDiarmid (1892–1978)
Scottish poet

In the case of some women, orgasms take quite a bit of time. Before
signing on with such a partner, make sure you are willing to lay aside,
say, the month of June, with sandwiches having to be brought in.

Bruce Jay Friedman

I FEEL LIKE A MILLION TONIGHT—
BUT ONE AT A TIME.

Mae West (1892–1980)
American actress

Women want more sex than men do. They want it more often, with more variation of technique, and they want it to last longer than you can possibly bear. They want it wilder, louder, and messier than you can ever imagine.

Shary Flenniken

My husband is German; every night I get dressed up
like Poland and he invades me.

Bette Midler (b. 1945)
American singer and actress

Eventually, all men come out of the bathroom dressed as a majorette.

Ernestyne White

As a rule, women would like to devote as much to foreplay and the sex act as men would like to devote to foreplay, the sex act, and building a garage.

Dave Barry (b. 1947)
American writer and humorist

A woman's appetite is twice that of a man's; her sexual desire,
four times; her intelligence, eight times.

Sanskrit proverb

There's very little advice in men's magazines, because men don't think there's a lot they don't know. Women do. Women want to learn. Men think, "I know what I'm doing, just show me somebody naked."

Jerry Seinfeld (b. 1954)
American actor and comedian

A man can sleep around, no questions asked, but if a woman makes nineteen or twenty mistakes, she's a tramp.

Joan Rivers (b. 1937)
American comedienne

The more a woman takes off her clothes, the more power she has and feminists hate strippers because modern professional women cannot stand the thought that their hard-won achievements can be out-weighed in an instant by a young hussy flashing a little tits and ass.

Camille Paglia (b. 1946)
American writer

Women complain about sex more often than men.
Their gripes fall into two categories; one, not enough; two, too much.

Ann Landers (b. 1918)
American advice columnist

You should marry for sex or money
and you're really lucky if you can get both.

Mae West (1892–1980)
American actress

Men are not women, and a man's balance
depends on the weight he carries between his legs.

James Baldwin (1861–1934)
American psychologist

The female sex drive is 60% vanity, 30% curiosity, and 10% physical. I didn't masturbate until I was seventeen—find me the man who can make that statement. My chief sexual fantasy involved showering together, and I was compelled to visualize it so that no water splashed on the floor and messed up my nice clean bathroom. Find me a man who would give a damn about the mess even in real life, never mind fantasy.

Florence King (b. 1936)
American writer

*We got new advice as to what motivated man to walk upright:
to free his hands for masturbation.*

Jane Wagner (b. 1935)
American writer and director

A woman occasionally is quite a serviceable substitute for masturbation. It takes an abundance of imagination to be sure.

Karl Kraus (1874–1936)
German writer and playwright

Feminism is a tool everyone should have, right next to the dildo.

Rebecca Walker (b. 1944)
Writer

Women over thirty are at their best,
but men over thirty are too old to recognize it.

Jean-Paul Belmondo (b. 1933)
French writer

March isn't the only thing that's in like a lion, out like a lamb.

Anonymous

I have always been principally interested in men for sex. I've always thought any sane woman would be a lover of women because loving men is such a mess. I have always wished I'd fall in love with a woman. Damn.

Germaine Greer (b. 1939)
English writer and feminist

Women are always trying to mix something up
with sex—religion, babies or hard case; it is only men who
long for sex separated out; without rings or strings.

Katherine Whitehorn (b. 1928)
English writer

THE ONLY ALLIANCE I WOULD MAKE WITH THE WOMEN'S LIBERATION MOVEMENT IS IN BED.

Abbie Hoffman (1936–1989)
American writer and activist

Intercourse is the pure, sterile, formal expression
of men's contempt for women.

Andrea Dworkin (b. 1946)
American writer and feminist

Once you know what women are like, men get kind of boring. I'm not trying to put them down. I mean I like them sometimes as people, but sexually they're dull.

Rita Mae Brown (b. 1944)
Writer

When a lady's erotic life is vexed God knows what is coming next.

Ogden Nash (1902–1971)
American poet and writer

It's a wise husband who keeps his own private chart
foreseeing his wife's premenstrual snits.

Gardner E. Lewis

You know why God is a man? Because if God was a woman she would have made sperm taste like chocolate.

Carrie Snow

I think it's disgusting. Sex has always been with us, but never so flamboyantly as it is today. I was known as the "kissless star." My leading men used to say, "What's the matter with me—do I have bad breath?" I said, "No, but I'm against kissing on the screen." In a way, a kiss is a promise, and I didn't want to create the wrong impression.

Mary Pickford (1894–1979)
Canadian actress

If marriage were only bed, we could have made it.

Marilyn Monroe (1926–1962)
American actress

Listen, Bond, it'd take more than Crabmeat Ravigote to get me into bed.

from *Diamonds Are Forever*

Last time I made love to my wife nothing was happening, so I said to her: "What's the matter? You can't think of anybody either?"

Rodney Dangerfield (b. 1921)
American comedian and actor

Sexual intercourse is a grossly overrated pastime; the position is undignified, the pleasure momentary, and the consequences utterly damnable.

Philip Dormer Stanhope, Earl of Chesterfield (1694–1773)
English writer and politician

A woman's ass is a man's business,
but a man's ass is his business and his alone.

Maryse Pelletier
20th-century Canadian writer

No man ever stuck his hand up your dress
looking for a library card.

Joan Rivers (b. 1937)
American comedienne

I'm a woman of the eighties. I can risk my life in armed combat,
I can have empty sex with strangers, and I want to be loved.

from *My Demon Lover*

When a man talks dirty to a woman, it's sexual harassment.
When a woman talks dirty to a man, it's $3.95 per hour.

Graffiti found in Memphis, Tennessee

As far as I'm concerned, being any gender is a drag.

Patti Smith (b. 1946)
American singer and poet

All this talk about sex, all this worry about sex—big deal.
The sun makes me happy. I eat good fish, he makes me happy.
I sleep with a good man, he makes me happy.

Melina Mercouri (b. 1925)
Greek actress and politician

Men always want to be a woman's first love. Women have a more subtle instinct: what they like is to be a man's last romance.

Oscar Wilde (1854–1900)
Irish poet and playwright

In love women are professionals, men are amateurs.

François Truffaut (1932–1984)
French director

Love is the same as like except you feel sexier. And more romantic. And also more annoyed when he talks with his mouth full. And you also resent it more when he interrupts you. And you also respect him less when he shows weakness. And furthermore, when you ask him to pick you up at the airport and he tells you he can't do it because he's busy, it's only when you love him that you hate him.

Judith Viorst (b. 1931)
American writer

Women in love are less ashamed than men. They have less to be ashamed of.

Ambrose Bierce (1842–1914)
American writer

Love diminishes the delicacy of women and increases that of men.

John Paul Richter (1763–1825)
German writer

A man in love is a stupid thing—he bores you stiff, in real life or anywhere else; but a woman in love is fascinating—she has a kind of aura.

Leslie Howard (1893–1943)
English actor

Women are happier in the love they inspire than that in which they feel; men are just the contrary.

De Beauchene

Men differ from women. You never see young men sitting around talking about their dream weddings.

Charles Cosart

Women speak easily of platonic love; but, while they appear to esteem it highly, there is not a single ribbon of their toilette that does not drive platonism from our hearts.

Auguste Ricard (1890–1980)
Investment banker

Women still remember the first kiss after men have forgotten the last.

Rémy de Gourmont (1858–1915)
French writer

To a woman the first kiss is the end of the beginning; to a man it is the beginning of the end.

Helen Rowland (1875–1950)
American writer

The only way to understand a woman is to love her— and then it isn't necessary to understand her.

Sydney Harris (1917–1986)
American writer

Women have considerable moral sense when they don't love a man. Mighty little when they do. With man, it's the opposite. If he doesn't care for a girl, he's without scruples. If he does care, he is likely to develop a moral code only the angels can live up to.

Mark Reed
19th-century playwright

A GUY KNOWS HE'S IN LOVE WHEN HE WANTS TO GROW OLD WITH A WOMAN. WHEN HE WANTS TO STAY WITH HER IN THE MORNING. . . . WHEN HE STARTS CALLING SEX "MAKING LOVE" AND AFTERWARD WANTS A GREAT BIG HUG. WHEN HE LOSES INTEREST IN THE CAR FOR A COUPLE OF DAYS. IT'S THAT SIMPLE, I SWEAR.—TIM ALLEN (B. 1953) AMERICAN ACTOR AND COMEDIAN

A man loses his sense of direction after four drinks;
a woman loses hers after four kisses.

H. L. Mencken (1888–1956)
American writer and editor

The trouble with women in love is that they are too generous; give too much. Men don't really like this. On the other hand if a woman is offhand they don't like that either. There is no answer.

Omar Sharif (b. 1932)
Egyptian-born American actor

When a woman has a love affair she goes into ecstasies;
a man goes into details.

Anonymous

Women are much more like each other than men; they have, in truth, but two passions, vanity and love; these are their universal characteristics.

Philip Dormer Stanhope, Earl of Chesterfield (1694–1773)
English writer and politician

To women, love is an occupation; to men, a preoccupation.

Lytton Strachey (1880–1932)
English biographer and historian

Men love and fall in love romantically,
women sensibly and rationally.

Nancy Chodrow
20th-century American professor and writer

It has been established that men fall in love faster than women.

Joyce Brothers (b. 1928)
American television personality and psychologist

What man sees in love is woman, what woman sees in man is love.

Arsene Houssaye (1815–1896)
French writer

Woman reaches love through friendship;
man reaches friendship through love.

Muhammad Hijazi

To be happy with a man you must understand him a lot and love him a little. To be happy with a woman you must love her a lot and not try to understand her at all.

Helen Rowland (1875–1950)
American writer

That's the nature of women . . . not to love when we love them, and to love when we love them not.

Miguel de Cervantes (1547–1616)
Spanish writer

A man falls in love through his eyes, a woman through her ears.

Woodrow Wyatt (b. 1918)
English writer

Whereas a woman's chief emotional need is active (i.e. to love), a man's prime emotional need is passive (i.e. to be appreciated and admired).

Phyllis Schlafly (b. 1924)
American writer

A woman is never in love with anyone she has always known—ever since she can remember; as a man often is. It is always some new fellow who strikes a girl.

George Eliot [Mary Ann Evans] (1819–1880)
English writer

Woman wants monogamy;
Man delights in novelty.
Love is woman's moon and sun;
Man has other forms of fun.
Woman lives but in her lord;
Count to ten and man is bored.

Dorothy Parker (1893–1967)
American writer

You see, a man can meet two, three, or four women and fall in love with all of them, and then, by a process of—er—interesting elimination, he is able to decide which he prefers; but a woman must decide purely on instinct, guesswork, if she wants to be considered nice.

from *Design for Living*

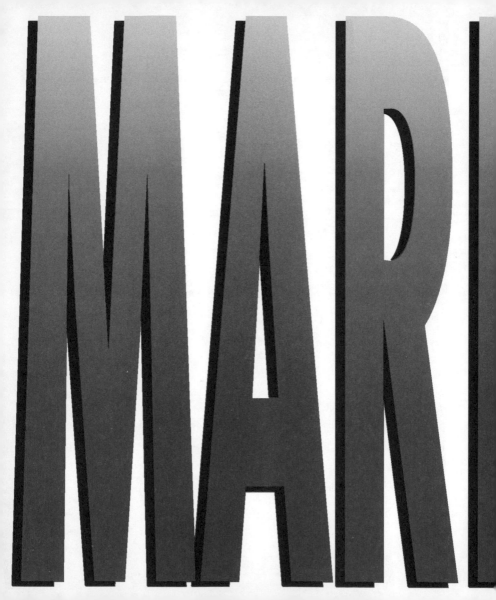

The reason husbands and wives do not understand each other
is because they belong to different sexes.

Dorothy Dix (1870–1951)
American journalist and writer

Sometimes I wonder if men and women really suit each other.
Perhaps they should live next door and just visit now and then.

Katharine Hepburn (b.1909)
American actress

Men and women—even man and wife—are foreigners.
Each has reserves that the other cannot enter into, nor understand.

Mark Twain [Samuel Clemens] (1835–1910)
American writer and humorist

The trouble with marriage is that, while every woman is at heart
a mother, every man is at heart a bachelor.

E. V. Lucas (1868–1938)
English writer

A woman marries a man expecting he will change, but he doesn't;
a man marries a woman expecting that she won't change and she does.

American saying

Men marry because they are tired;
woman because they are curious; both are disappointed.

Oscar Wilde (1854–1900)
Irish poet and playwright

A woman worries about the future until she gets a husband,
while a man never worries about the future until he gets a wife.

Anonymous

Men marry to make an end; women to make a beginning.

Alexandre Dumas (1824–1895)
French playwright

The woman who does not marry makes a blunder
that can only be compared to that of the man who does.

Anonymous

If you want a recipe for depression, have a woman
get married and have young children. If you want a recipe
for male well-being, have him do the same.

Neil Jacobsen (b. 1930)
American psychologist

Man conceives fortune, but woman conducts it.

Benjamin Disraeli (1804–1881)
English politician and writer

Marriage is a condition most women aspire to and most men submit to.

Anonymous

A man who marries a woman to educate her falls a victim
to the same fallacy as the woman who marries a man to reform him.

Elbert Hubbard (1856–1915)
American writer and editor

Marriage is the price men pay for sex,
and sex is the price women pay for marriage.

Anonymous

Marriage was all a woman's idea, and for man's acceptance
of the pretty yoke it becomes us to be grateful.

Phyllis McGinley (1905–1978)
American poet and writer

Marriage is obsolete: a trap for both sexes where, too often, the man becomes a boss and the woman becomes a shrew.

Catharine Deneuve (b. 1943)
French actress

In a happy marriage it is the wife who provides the climate, the husband the landscape.

Gerald Brenan (1894–1987)
English writer

Any man with any style at all can make a mess of his love life, and any woman with any gumption at all can make a shambles of her marriage.

from *Reuben, Reuben*

Men who love to command must be especially careful not to marry imperious, women's rights women; while those who willingly "obey orders" need just such. A timid woman should never marry a hesitating man, lest, like frightened children, each keep perpetually re-alarming the other by imaginary fears.

Russel Crouse, quoting Victorian etiquette advice

A woman will always cherish the memory of the man
who wanted to marry her; a man, of the woman who didn't.

Viola Brothers Shore (1891–1970)
American dramatist

One of the great reasons why so many husbands and wives make a
shipwreck of their lives together is because a man is always seeking
happiness, while a woman is on a perpetual still hunt for trouble.

Dorothy Dix (1870–1951)
American journalist and writer

When women are at the height of their beauty, power, and exercise,
we call it marriage. When men are at the height of their success,
power, and exercise, we call it a midlife crisis . . . "Sow your wild
oats," for a man, means "get your primary fantasy out of your sys-
tem." The equivalent, for a woman, would be "sow your domestic
oats"–get married.

Warren Farrell (b. 1943)
American psychologist and writer

If you're looking for monogamy, you'd better marry a swan.

from *Heartburn*

It is ridiculous to think you can spend your entire life with one person. Three is about the right number. Yes, I imagine three husbands would do it.

Clare Booth Luce (1903–1987)
American writer and politician

Marriage has driven more than one man to sex.

Peter De Vries (1910–1995)
American writer and editor

The desire to get married, which—I regret to say—I believe is basic and primal in women, is followed almost immediately by an equally basic and primal urge—which is to be single again.

Nora Ephron (b. 1941)
American writer and screenwriter

Marriages don't last. When I meet a guy, the first question I ask myself is: Is this the man I want my children to spend their weekends with?

Rita Rudner (b. 1956)
American comedienne and actress

In Biblical times, a man could have as many wives as he could afford. Just like today.

Abigail Van Buren (b. 1918)
American advice columnist

It takes a man twenty-five years to learn to be married;
it's a wonder women have patience to wait for it.

Clarence B. Kelland (1881–1964)
American writer

It is a mistake for a taciturn, serious-minded woman to marry a jovial
man, but not for a serious-minded man to marry a lighthearted woman.

Johann Wolfgang von Goethe (1749–1832)
German poet and writer

What women look for in a man: breathing, IQ over 80, weight under 550 lbs., fewer than six ex-wives. What men look for in a woman: Pia Zadora as she was ten years ago.

C. E. Crimmins
20th-century American writer

Marriage is like a bank account. You put it in,
you take it out, you lose interest.

Irwin Corey (b. 1912)
American comedian and actor

When a man declares, "I am sure of my wife," it means
he is sure of his wife. But when a woman declares,
"I am sure of my husband," it means she is sure of herself.

Francis de Croisset (1877–1937)
French playwright

There are two times when a man doesn't understand a woman—before marriage and after marriage.

Anonymous

Marriage is a custom brought about by women who then proceed to live off men and destroy them, completely enveloping the man in a destructive cocoon or eating them away like a poisonous fungus on a tree.

from *Beverly Hills People*

**Two days are the best of a man's wedded life,
The days when he marries and buries his wife.**

Hipponax
6th-century B.C. Greek writer

No man should marry until he has studied anatomy
and dissected at least one woman.

Honore de Balzac (1799–1850)
French writer

*You always hear women say that all the best men are married or gay.
Funny, but you'd never hear a man say that about women.*

Jim Mullen (b. 1945)
Musician

I'm old-fashioned. I like two sexes. All of a sudden
I don't like being married to what's known as a "new woman."
I want a wife, not a competition.

from *Adam's Rib*

When women hold off from marrying men, we call it independence.
When men hold off from marrying women, we call it fear of commitment.

Warren Farrell (b. 1943)
American psychologist and writer

*I think it can be stated without denial that no man ever saw
a man he would be willing to marry if he were a woman.*

George Gibbs (b. 1926)
American writer

Men are horribly tedious when they are good husbands,
and abominably conceited when they are not.

Oscar Wilde (1854–1900)
Irish poet and playwright

**Only two things are necessary to keep one's wife happy. One is to let
her think she is having her own way, and the other is to let her have it.**

Lyndon B. Johnson (1908–1973)
American president

If men knew how women pass the time when they are alone, they'd never marry.

O. Henry [William Sydney Porter] (1862–1910)
American writer

Wives are people who feel they don't dance enough.

Groucho Marx (1890–1977)
American comedian and actor

All men make mistakes, but married men find out about them sooner.

Red Skelton (b. 1913)
American comedian and actor

A man should sleep sometime between lunch and dinner in order to be at his best in the evening when he joins his wife and friends at dinner. My wife and I tried two or three times in the last forty years to have breakfast together, but it was so disagreeable we had to stop.

Winston Churchill (1874–1965)
English statesman and writer

I WILL TELL YOU THE REAL SECRET OF HOW TO STAY MARRIED. KEEP THE CAVE CLEAN. THEY WANT THE CAVE CLEAN AND SPOTLESS. AIR-CONDITIONED, IF POSSIBLE. SHARPEN HIS SPEAR, AND STICK IT IN HIS HAND WHEN HE GOES OUT IN THE MORNING TO SPEAR THAT BEAR; AND WHEN THE BEAR CHASES HIM, CONSOLE HIM WHEN HE COMES HOME AT NIGHT, AND TELL HIM WHAT A BIG MAN HE IS, AND THEN HIDE THE SPEAR SO HE DOESN'T FALL OVER IT AND STAB HIMSELF.—JEROME CHODOROV AND JOSEPH FIELDS

A loving wife will do anything for her husband
except stop criticizing and trying to improve him.

J. B. Priestley (1733–1804)
English scientist

Marriage is the way a man finds out
what kind of husband his wife would have preferred.

Anonymous

Women will never be as successful as men
because they have no wives to advise them.

Dick Van Dyke (b. 1925)
American actor and comedian

Married men live longer than single men.
But married men are a lot more willing to die.

Johnny Carson (b. 1925)
American talk show host

My wife gives good headache.

Rodney Dangerfield (b. 1921)
American comedian and actor

Any married man should forget his mistakes—no use two people remembering the same thing.

Duane Dewel (b. 1901)
American writer

The fundamental trouble with marriage is that it shakes a man's confidence in himself, and so greatly diminishes his general competence and effectiveness. His habit of mind becomes that of a commander who has lost a decisive and calamitous battle. He never quite trusts himself thereafter.

H. L. Mencken (1880–1956)
American writer and editor

The majority of husbands remind me
of an orangutan trying to play the violin.

Honore de Balzac (1799–1850)
French writer

**Women, deceived by men, want to marry them;
it is a kind of revenge as good as any other.**

Philippe de Remi
13th-century French writer

To marry a woman you love and who loves you
is to lay a wager with her as to who will stop loving the other first.

Alfred Capus (1858–1922)
French writer

I couldn't see tying myself down with a middle-aged woman
with four children, even though the woman was my wife
and the children were my own.

Joseph Heller (b. 1923)
American writer and playwright

*Am I not a man? And is not a man stupid?
I'm a man, so I married. Wife, children, house,
everything, the full catastrophe.*

from *Zorba the Greek*

The only thing that holds a marriage together is the husband being big enough to step back and see where the wife is wrong.

from *All in the Family*

By all means marry; if you get a good wife, you'll become happy; if you get a bad one, you'll become a philosopher.

Socrates (c. 470–399 B.C.)
Greek philosopher

I was married by a judge. I should have asked for a jury.

George Burns (1896–1996)
American comedian and actor

A man has no business to marry a woman who can't make him miserable. It means she can't make him happy.

Proverb

Marriage is much more necessary to a man than to a woman; for he is much less able to supply himself with domestic comforts.

Samuel Johnson (1709–1784)
English writer

My wife was too beautiful for words, but not for arguments.

John Barrymore (1882–1942)
American actor

Marriage is about the most expensive way for the average man to get laundry done.

Burt Reynolds (b. 1936)
American actor

We sleep in separate rooms, we have dinner apart,
we take separate vacations—we're doing everything
we can to keep our marriage together.

Rodney Dangerfield (b. 1921)
American comedian and actor

Marriage is the best magician there is. In front of your eyes,
it can change an exciting, cute little dish into a boring dishwasher.

Ryan O'Neal (b. 1941)
American actor

No matter who you marry, you wake up married to someone else.

from *Guys and Dolls*

Every good wife should commit a few infidelities
to keep her husband in countenance.

George Bernard Shaw (1856–1950)
English playwright and critic

Why can't somebody invent something for us to marry besides women?

from *The Flintstones*

We want playmates we can own.

Jules Feiffer (b. 1929)
American cartoonist

Anyone who thinks marriage is a fifty-fifty proposition
doesn't understand women, or fractions.

Danny Thomas (1914–1991)
American actor

Men have a much better time of it than women.
For one thing, they marry later. For another thing, they die earlier.

H. L. Mencken (1880–1956)
American writer and editor

Sexiness wears thin after a while and beauty fades, but to be married to a man who makes you laugh every day, ah, now that's a real treat!

Joanne Woodward (b. 1930)
American actress

People are always asking couples whose marriage has endured at least a quarter of a century for their secret for success. Actually, it is no secret at all. I am a forgiving woman. Long ago, I forgave my husband for not being Paul Newman.

Erma Bombeck (1927–1996)
American writer

If men acted after marriage as they do during courtship, there would be fewer divorces—and more bankruptcies.

Frances Rodman (b. 1934)
American writer

DEAR ABBY: What factor do you think is the most essential factor if a woman is to have a lasting marriage?—Dotty.

DEAR DOTTY: A lasting husband.

Abigail Van Buren (b. 1918)
American advice columnist

A husband is what is left of the lover after the nerve has been extracted.

Helen Rowland (1875–1950)
American writer

If you never want to see a man again, say "I love you,
I want to marry you, I want to have children"—they leave skid marks.

Rita Rudner (b. 1956)
American comedienne and actress

Mahatma Gandhi was what wives wish their husbands were: thin, tan, and moral.

Anonymous

Throughout history, females have picked providers for males.
Males pick anything.

Margaret Mead (1901–1978)
American anthropologist

For men, marriage is regarded as a station; for women, as a vocation.

Suzanne LaFollette (1893–1983)
American politician and writer

When a couple gets married, a man usually—and willingly—steps aside while his wife throws herself into transforming their dwelling into a home. Then, when everything is just so, the husband brings out his most prized possession. This is usually something like a lava lamp, an orange recliner or a stuffed dead animal. And it is always non-negotiable.

Nancy Kennedy

Some husbands are living proof that a woman can take a joke.

Anonymous

Marrying a man is like buying something you've been admiring for a long time in a shop window. You may love it when you get it home, but it doesn't always go with everything else in the house.

Jean Kerr (b. 1923)
American writer and playwright

The first time you buy a house you see how pretty the paint is and buy it. The second time you look to see if the basement has termites. It's the same with men.

Lupe Velez (1910–1944)
Mexican actress

Two women. One when alone is exactly the same as she is in company, the other in company exactly what she is when she is alone. The latter holds herself badly in public, the former puts on an evening dress when she dines by herself. One should marry neither.

Paul Valéry (1871–1945)
French poet and critic

Just because we're married to men doesn't mean we've got anything in common with them.

from *I Love Lucy*

Husbands are like cars: all are good the first year.

Channing Pollack

Before marriage a man will lie awake all night thinking about something you said; after marriage he'll fall asleep before you finish saying it.

Helen Rowland (1875–1950)
American writer

A husband is really broken in when he can understand every word his wife isn't saying.

Shannon Fif

Many women feel it is natural to consult with their partners at every turn, while many men automatically make more decisions without consulting their partners.

Deborah Tannen (b. 1945)
American linguist and writer

Women speak because they wish to speak, whereas a man speaks only when driven to speech by something outside himself—like, for instance, he can't find any clean socks.

Jean Kerr (b. 1923)
American writer and playwright

I married beneath me—all women do.

Nancy Astor (1879–1964)
English politician

You marry the man of your dreams, but fifteen years later you're married to a reclining chair that burps.

Roseanne (b. 1953)
American actress and comedienne

It is a waste of time trying to change a man's character.
You have to accept a husband as he is.

Elizabeth II (b. 1926)
Queen of England

Why get married and make one man miserable when I can stay single and make thousands miserable?

Carrie Snow

If you don't get married you'll never have a good man.
On the other hand, if you ain't married, you don't need one.

Gladiola Montana

I never married because there was no need. I have three pets at home which answer the same purpose as a husband. I have a dog that growls every morning, a parrot which swears all afternoon, and a cat which comes home late at night.

Marie Corelli (1855–1924)
English writer

A man likes his wife to be just clever enough to comprehend his cleverness, and just stupid enough to admire it.

Israel Zangwill (1864–1926)
English writer and playwright

For women, the only sane way to live through it is without closure. Marriage to a lover is fatal: lovers are not husbands. More important, husbands are not lovers. The compulsion to find a lover and husband in a single person has doomed more women to misery than any other illusion.

Carolyn G. Heilbrun (b. 1926)
American writer

Husbands are chiefly good lovers when they are betraying their wives.

Marilyn Monroe (1926–1962)
American actress

Husbands are like fires. They go out if unattended.

Zsa Zsa Gabor (b. 1917)
Hungarian-born American actress

Husbands are awkward things to deal with;
even keeping them in hot water will not make them tender.

Mary Buckley
20th-century American writer and lecturer

There is so little difference between husbands that you might as well keep the first.

Adela Rogers St. Johns (1894–1988)
American writer and journalist

I have yet to hear a man ask for advice
on how to combine marriage and a career.

Gloria Steinem (b. 1934)
American writer and feminist

Husbands think we should know where everything is—like the uterus is a tracking device. He asks me, "Roseanne, do you have any Cheetos left?" Like he can't go over to that sofa cushion himself.

Roseanne (b. 1953)
American actress and comedienne

Why does a woman work ten years to change a man's habits
and then complain that he's not the man she married?

Barbra Streisand (b. 1942)
American singer, actress, and director

Women do generally manage to love the guys they marry. They manage to love the guy they marry more than they manage to marry the guy they love.

Clare Booth Luce (1903–1987)
American writer and politician

A real woman has a special attitude toward money. If she earns it,
it is hers; if her husband earns it, it is theirs.

Joyce Jillson (b. 1950)
American writer and actress

Husbands should be like Kleenex, soft, clean, and disposable.

Madeline Kahn (b. 1942)
American actress

Trust your husband, adore your husband,
and get as much as you can in your own name.

Joan Rivers (b. 1937)
American comedienne

When a man brings his wife flowers for no reason—there's a reason.

Molly McGee and Marion Jordan

When he's late for dinner, I know he's either having an affair or is lying dead in the street. I always hope it's the street.

Jessica Tandy (1909–1994)
English-born American actress

My husband will never chase another woman.
He's too fine, he's too decent, he's too old.

Gracie Allen (1906–1964)
American comedienne

The war between the sexes is the only one
in which both sides regularly sleep with the enemy.

Quentin Crisp (b. 1908)
English writer

Between men and women there is no friendship possible. There is passion, enmity, worship, love, but no friendship.

Oscar Wilde (1854–1900)
Irish poet and playwright

Who can dispute that the war between the sexes
boils down to who gets to sit behind the wheel?

Anemona Hartocollis

Ever since Eve game Adam the apple, there has been
a misunderstanding between the sexes about gifts.

Nan Robertson (b. 1926)
American writer

In the battle of the sexes, every woman has her curves
and every man his angles.

Anonymous

The best part about married life is the fights.
The rest is merely so-so.

Thornton Wilder (1897–1975)
American writer and dramatist

There are three things a woman can make out of almost nothing—a salad, a hat, and a quarrel.

John Barrymore (1882–1942)
American actor

If it weren't for marriage, men and women
would have to fight with total strangers.

Anonymous

All married couples should learn the art of battle as they should learn the art of making love. Good battle is objective and honest—never vicious and cruel. Good battle is healthy and constructive, and brings to a marriage the principle of equal partnership.

Ann Landers (b. 1918)
American advice columnist

In the battle of the sexes, men are more deceitful,
but women are more deceptive.

Anonymous

In the sex-war thoughtlessness is the weapon of the male,
vindictiveness of the female.

Cyril Connolly (1903–1974)
English critic and writer

Getting divorced just because you don't love a man is almost as silly as getting married just because you do.

Zsa Zsa Gabor (b. 1917)
Hungarian-born American actress

The only way a man can get the better of a woman in an argument
is to let her keep on talking after she has won it.

Richard Atteridge (1886–1938)
American playwright

A WOMAN HAS THE LAST WORD IN ANY ARGUMENT. ANYTHING A MAN SAYS AFTER THAT IS THE BEGINNING OF A NEW ARGUMENT.

Anonymous

*A woman knows how to keep quiet when she is right,
whereas a man, when he is right, will keep on talking.*

Malcolm de Chazal (b. 1902)
French writer

The battle between the sexes is like that between landlord
and tenant: both sides agree that damage has occurred;
each feels that the other should pay for it.

Mignon McLaughlin
20th-century American writer and editor

MARRIAGE IS NOT A MAN'S IDEA. A WOMAN MUST HAVE THOUGHT OF IT. YEARS AGO SOME GUY SAID, "LET ME GET THIS STRAIGHT, HONEY. I CAN'T SLEEP WITH ANYONE ELSE FOR THE REST OF MY LIFE, AND IF THINGS DON'T WORK OUT, YOU GET TO KEEP HALF MY STUFF? WHAT A GREAT IDEA."—BOBBY SLAYTON

Even the deepest love doesn't stop a marriage
from being a constant struggle for control.

Bill Cosby (b. 1937)
American actor and comedian

When men and women agree, it is only in their conclusions;
their reasons are always different.

George Santayana (1863–1952)
Spanish-born American poet and philosopher

God made man. God made woman. And when God found that men
could not get along with women, God invented Mexico.

Larry Storch (b. 1923)
American actor and comedian

Marriage is really tough because
you have to deal with feelings and lawyers.

Richard Pryor (b. 1940)
American actor and comedian

I don't believe man is woman's natural enemy. Perhaps his lawyer is.

Shana Alexander (b. 1925)
American writer and lecturer

In marriage, as in war, it is permitted to take every advantage of the enemy.

Douglas Jerrold (1893–1964)
American writer

Never go to bed mad. Stay up and fight.

Phyllis Diller (b. 1917)
American comedienne

My attitude toward men who mess around is simple:
If you find 'em, kill 'em.

Loretta Lynne (b. 1935)
American singer

If women were as big as men, we'd be in real trouble.

Terry McDonald

There will always be a battle between the sexes
because men and women want different things.
Men want women and women want men.

George Burns (1896–1996)
American comedian and actor

Meaningful relationships between men and women don't last. You
see, there's a chemical in our bodies that makes it so that we all get
on each other's nerves sooner or later.

Diane Keaton (b. 1946)
American actress

Do I ever think about divorce? Never. Murder? All the time.

Sybil Thorndike (1882–1976)
English actress

It is true that I never should have married, but I didn't want to live
without a man. Brought up to respect the conventions, love had to
end in marriage. I'm afraid it did.

Bette Davis (1908–1989)
American actress

If divorce has increased one thousand percent, don't blame the women's movement. Blame our obsolete sex roles on which our marriages are based.

Betty Friedan (b. 1921)
American writer

The only solid and lasting peace between a man and his wife
is doubtless a separation.

Philip Dormer Stanhope, Earl of Chesterfield (1694–1773)
English writer and politician

The difference between a divorce and a legal separation
is that a legal separation gives a husband time to hide his money.

Johnny Carson (b. 1925)
American talk show host

One of the surest signs that a woman is in love
is when she divorces her husband.

Dolly Parton (b. 1946)
American singer and actress

You never really know a man until you have divorced him.

Zsa Zsa Gabor (b. 1917)
Hungarian-born American actress

You don't know anything about a woman until you meet her in court.

Norman Mailer (b. 1923)
American writer

We're the weaker sex! We don't live as long as women; we get more heart attacks, more strokes, more prostate trouble. I say, it's time for a change. I say, let's let them give us money! Let's live off them for a while.

from *Dirty Rotten Scoundrels*

This fundamental truth—that women are not just men who can have babies and men are not just women who spike footballs—gives marriage its dynamics, its delights, and its divorce.

Bill Cosby (b. 1937)
American actor and comedian

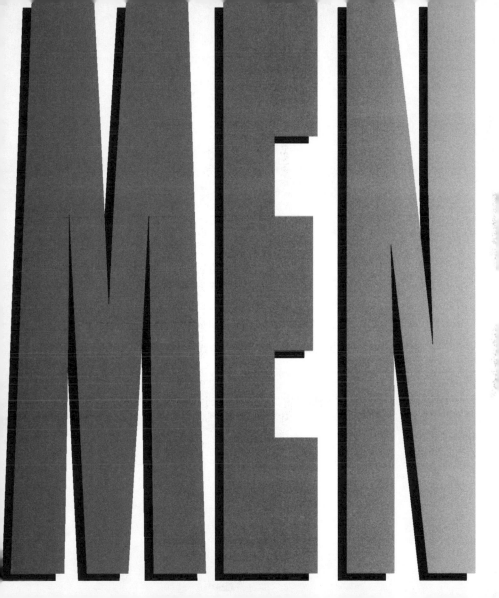

Men have more problems than women.
In the first place, they have to put up with women.

Françoise Sagan (b. 1936)
French writer

Men are pigs and we're tired of apologizing for it.

Bill Maher
20th-century American comedian and talk show host

Men are pigs; I don't care how nice they seem.

from *Single White Female*

Men are superior to women. For one thing, they can urinate from a speeding car.

Will Durst (1873–1951)
Canadian writer

All men are not slimy warthogs. Some men are silly giraffes,
some woebegone puppies, some insecure frogs. But if one is not careful,
those slimy warthogs can ruin it for all the others.

Cynthia Heimel (b. 1947)
American writer and playwright

**Although man has learned through evolution to walk
in an upright position, his eyes still swing from limb to limb.**

Margaret Schooley

99% of men give the other 1% a bad name.

Anonymous

As long as you know that most men are children,
you know everything.

Coco Chanel (1882–1971)
French fashion designer

Man is the missing link between the ape and the human being.

Anonymous

Every man is a failed boy.

John Updike (b. 1932)
American writer

Every fool . . . can make a baby, but only a man can raise his children.

from *Boyz N the Hood*

Men get opinions as boys learn to spell.
By reiteration chiefly.

Elizabeth Barrett Browning (1806–1861)
English poet

There is no such thing as a man . . . Just a little boy in a man's body.

Elvis Presley (1935–1977)
American singer and actor

I'm still a little boy, and I don't know a man who isn't.

Jonathan Winters (b. 1925)
American comedian and actor

A man's home may seem to be his castle on the outside;
inside, it is more often his nursery.

Clare Booth Luce (1903–1987)
American writer and politician

Men are beasts and even beasts don't behave as they do.

Brigitte Bardot (b. 1934)
French actress

Man at ten is an animal, at twenty a lunatic, at thirty a failure, at forty a fraud, and at fifty a criminal. Perhaps he becomes a criminal because he never ceased to be an animal.

Kakuzo Okakura (1862–1913)
Japanese writer

Whatever happened to the strong silent type? Today's man talks, talks, talks till we're blue in the face. And I fear there's no undoing the damage. The new old saying? Boys will be noise.

Nina Malkin

Men are what their mothers made them.

Ralph Waldo Emerson (1803–1882)
American writer and poet

A good man doesn't happen. They have to be created by us women. A guy is a lump like a doughnut. So, first you gotta get rid of all the stuff his mom did to him. And then you gotta get rid of all that macho crap that they pick up from the beer commercials. And then there's my personal favorite, the male ego.

Roseanne (b. 1953)
American actress and comedienne

The standard Western adult male is rendered incapable of being comfortable with emotional expression . . . being quite incapable of understanding what it is like to be someone else.

Janet Daley (b. 1944)
English writer

The classic function of the "warrior" helped men throughout history achieve a sense of confidence they needed in order to cope with women.

Page Smith (b. 1917)
American historian

By the time a man is thirty-five he knows that the images of the right man, the tough man, the true man which he received in high school do not work in life.

Robert Bly (b. 1926)
American poet

When it comes to women, men are idiots. They don't know what they want, and so they never want, permanently, what they get. They want a cream cake that is at the same time ham and eggs and at the same time porridge. They are fools. If only women weren't bound by fate to play up to them.

D. H. Lawrence (1885–1930)
English writer

God created man and, finding him not sufficiently alone, gave him a companion to make him feel his solitude more keenly.

Paul Valéry (1871–1945)
French poet and critic

No man, as a general rule, shows his soul to another man;
he shows it only to a woman.

Lafcadio Hearn (1850–1904)
American writer

When I wake up in the morning, I think of me first and then my wife and then my children. I'd like to meet the guy that can honestly admit he does differently.

Jerry Lewis (b. 1926)
American comedian and actor

Men say women can't be trusted too far—
women say men can't be trusted too near.

Croft M. Pentz
American writer and minister

Men are those creatures with two legs and eight arms.

Jayne Mansfield (1932–1967)
American actress

A man is two people, himself and his cock. A man always takes his friend to the party. Of the two, the friend is nicer, being able to show his feelings.

Beryl Bainbridge (b. 1933)
English writer

Men! You can't live with them and can't: 1. Dip them in batter tempura; 2. Use them for collateral on a loan; 3. Put in new batteries.

Nicole Hollander

Man is born into the world as a pig and is civilized by women.

John David Lodge (b. 1935)
Writer

A man chases a woman until she catches him.

Anonymous

Man is to be held only by the *slightest* chains; with the idea that he can break them a pleasure, he submits to them in sport.

Maria Edgeworth (1767–1849)
English writer

Men say they love independence in a woman, but they don't
waste a second demolishing it brick by brick.

Candice Bergen (b. 1946)
American actress

Never underestimate a man's ability to underestimate a woman.

from *V.I. Warshawski*

Men are gluttons for punishment. They fight over women
for the chance to fight with them.

Vincent Price (1911–1993)
American actor

Men are always doomed to be duped . . . They are always
wooing goddesses, and marrying mere mortals.

Washington Irving (1783–1859)
American writer

Men never learn anything about women,
but they have a lot of fun trying.

Olin Miller

If you women knew what we were thinking, you'd never stop slapping us.

Larry Miller (b. 1921)
American broadcasting executive

If a woman hasn't met the right man by the time
she's twenty-four, she may be lucky.

Deborah Kerr
20th-century Scottish-born American actress

*A man is an accessory, like a pair of earrings. It may finish the outfit,
but you don't really need it to keep you warm.*

Rosemary Mittelmark

Why are women so much more interesting to men
than men are to women?

Virginia Woolf (1882–1941)
English writer and critic

Men know that if a woman had to choose between catching a fly
ball and saving an infant's life, she would probably save the infant's
life, without even considering whether there were men on base.

Dave Barry (b. 1947)
American writer and humorist

Why we oppose votes for men . . . Because men are too emotional to vote. Their conduct at baseball games and political conventions show this, while their innate tendency to appeal to force renders them particularly unfit for the task of government.

Alice Duer Miller (1874–1942)
American writer

Males are a vast breeding experiment run by females.

Irven De Vore (b. 1934)
American writer and anthropologist

I regard men as a pleasant pastime but no more dependable than the British weather.

Anna Raeburn
English psychotherapist

The great truth is that women actually like men, and men can never believe it.

Isabel Patterson

I like a man who's good, but not too good.
The good die young and I hate a dead one.

Mae West (1892–1980)
American actress

The only place men want depth in a woman is in her décolletage.

Attributed to Zsa Zsa Gabor (b. 1917)
Hungarian-born American actress

He is a half-dead, unresponsive lump—consequently he is at best an utter bore . . . eaten up with guilt, shame, fears, and insecurities and obtaining, if he's lucky, a barely perceptible physical feeling; the male is, nonetheless, obsessed with screwing.

Valerie Solan

WHY DO MEN HAVE NIPPLES?

Silver Rose

What do men want? Men want a boy's body with tits on it.

Germaine Greer (b. 1939)
English writer and feminist

The male sex, as a sex, does not universally appeal to me. I find the men today less manly; but a woman of my age is not in a position to know exactly how manly they are.

Katharine Hepburn (b. 1909)
American actress

BEWARE OF MEN ON AIRPLANES. THE MINUTE A MAN REACHES THIRTY THOUSAND FEET, HE IMMEDIATELY BECOMES CONSUMED BY DISTASTEFUL SEXUAL FANTASIES WHICH INVOLVE DOING UNCOMFORTABLE THINGS IN THOSE TINY TOILETS. THESE MEN SHOULD NOT BE ENCOURAGED; THEIR FANTASIES ARE SADLY LOW-RENT AND UNIMAGINATIVE. AFFECT AN ALOOF, COOL DEMEANOR AS SOON AS ANY MAN TRIES TO DRAW YOU OUT. UNLESS, OF COURSE, HE'S THE PILOT.—CYNTHIA HEIMEL (B. 1947) AMERICAN WRITER AND PLAYWRIGHT

You know why the world is in such a mess? Men.
It's a man's world and all men are alike.

from *Come Fly with Me*

Men are nothing but lazy lumps of drunken flesh. They crowd you
in bed, get you all worked up, and then before you can say "Is that
all there is?" that's all there is.

from *Taxi*

There are men I could spend eternity with. But not this life.

Kathleen Norris (1880–1966)
American writer

Men read maps better than women because only men
can understand the concept of an inch equaling a hundred miles.

Roseanne (b. 1953)
American actress and comedienne

A man is like a phonograph with half-a-dozen records. You soon
get tired of them all; and yet you have to sit at a table whilst he
reels them off to every new visitor.

George Bernard Shaw (1856–1950)
English playwright and critic

You have to be very fond of men. Very, very fond. You have to be very fond of them to love them. Otherwise they are simply unbearable.

Marguerite Duras (b. 1914)
French writer and filmmaker

I like men to behave like men—strong and childish.

Françoise Sagan (b. 1935)
French writer

Men are frightened by women's humor because they think that when women are alone they're making fun of men. This is perfectly true. But they think we're making fun of their equipment when in fact there are so many more interesting things to make fun of— such as their value systems. Or the way they act when they're sick.

Nicole Hollander

Men go to seed early. They go to bars and sit in front of their TVs. Men at forty already have pot bellies.

from *Moscow Does Not Believe in Tears*

The more I see of men, the more I like dogs.

Germaine de Stael (1766–1817)
French writer

A man—despite some similarities—is not like dog droppings. For one thing, he's probably too big to just step over.

Dorian Yeager

Men are no good at playing dumb because most of the time they're not playing . . . To women, we are like big dogs that talk.

Larry Miller (b. 1943)
American broadcasting executive

MEN ARE ANIMALS, BUT THEY MAKE GREAT PETS.

Bumper sticker

They're the only animals who have money and buy champagne.

from *Song of Songs*

Talking with a man is like trying to saddle a cow. You work like hell, but what's the point.

Gladys Upham

If they can put one man on the moon, why can't they put them all?

Anonymous

I require three things in a man.
He must be handsome, ruthless, and stupid.

Dorothy Parker (1893–1967)
American writer

Why did nature create Man? Was it to show she is big enough to make mistakes, or was it pure ignorance?

Holbrook Jackson (1874–1948)
English writer

If men can run the world, why can't they stop wearing neckties?
How intelligent is it to start the day by tying a little noose around your neck?

Linda Ellerbee (b. 1944)
American broadcast journalist

There is nothing that disgusts a man
like getting beaten at chess by a woman.

Charles Dudley Warner (1829–1900)
American writer and editor

Man without woman would be as stupid
a game as playing checkers alone.

Josh Billings [Henry Wheller Shaw] (1818–1885)
American writer

Man forgives woman anything save the wit to outwit him.

Minna Antrim (b. 1856–1950)
American writer

Men hate to be misunderstood,
and to be understood makes them furious.

Edgar Saltus (1885–1921)
American writer

*If men knew all that women think,
they would be twenty times more audacious.*

Alphonse Karr (1808–1890)
French writer and editor

The tragedy of machismo is that a man is never quite man enough.

Germaine Greer (b. 1939)
English writer and feminist

You have to understand that men can be awfully sluggish about making decisions of the heart. Remember, please, that evolution is a slow process. Amphibians didn't exactly decide to become reptiles. One day, one brave, scaly green guy took a long walk on land and cautiously said, "Okay, okay, I can handle this." That's how life science is.

Stephanie Brush (b. 1954)
American writer

Why do men go to war? Because the women are watching. . . . Male displays and bravado evolved as a reproductive strategy to impress females. Machismo is biologically based and says in effect: "I have good genes. Let me mate."

Irven De Vore (b. 1934)
American writer and anthropologist

There should be a theme park based on
the male ego . . . only there's not enough land.

Margo Kaufman (b. 1939)
Hollywood correspondent

Men have been taught to deal only with what they understand. This is what they respect. They know that somewhere feeling and knowledge are important, so they keep women around to do their feeling for them, like ants do aphids.

Audre Lorde (1934–1992)
American poet and feminist

Every man sees a little of himself in Rhett Butler.

Ted Turner (b. 1938)
American businessman

Aren't men full of shit?

from *Shirley Valentine*

Women are good listeners, but it's a waste of time telling your troubles to a man unless there's something you want him to do.

Mignon McLaughlin
20th-century American writer and editor

A man cannot be very kind unless he is also very strong.

Shirley Hufstedler

The best way to find out if a man has done something is to advise him to do it. He will not be able to resist boasting that he has done without being advised.

Comtesse Diane (1554–1620)

The best way to get most husbands to do something is to suggest that perhaps they're too old to do it.

Shirley MacLaine (b. 1934)
American actress

Men build bridges and throw railroads across deserts, and yet they contend successfully that the job of sewing on a button is beyond them. Accordingly, they don't have to sew buttons.

Heywood Broun (1888–1939)
American writer

A woman works her ass off all the time. The guy does two things around the house and he's got to show her. "Honey, look! I fixed the screen! And look over there: I washed my dish!"

Diane Ford

If there is anything disagreeable going on, men are sure to get out of it.

Jane Austen (1775–1817)
English writer

Women want mediocre men, and men are working
hard to be as mediocre as possible.

Margaret Mead (1901–1978)
American anthropologist

I fear nothing so much as a man who is witty all day long.

Madame de Sevigne (1626–1696)
French writer

Woman's make-believe is only on the skin—not under it. Man, on the other hand, plays the astute game naively. Tell him he is a perpetual boy and he tumbles over himself to admit the charge that he has never grown up. Picture him as a sort of baboon in accidental captivity, he smiles benignly and rubs imaginary whiskers. Give him the wise head of a Moses or a Solomon on the body of an innocent cherub, and he is satisfied. All he asks is to remain unknown, apparently simple, easily explained, while woman is camouflaged as the eternal puzzle.

Florence Guy Seabury (1881–1951)
American writer

All men are frauds. The only difference between them is that some admit it. I myself deny it.

H. L. Mencken (1880–1956)
American writer and editor

Men, when they are lost, instinctively fall back on their built-in navigational skills, honed from far-off days of tracking large prey miles from home. Women, by contrast, tend to find their way by the simpler methods of remembering local landmarks or even asking help from strangers.

Nicholas Wade (b. 1943)
American writer

What's wrong with you men? Would hair stop growing on your chest if you asked directions somewhere?

Erma Bombeck (1927–1996)
American writer

Men are very queer animals—a mixture of horse-nervousness, ass-stubbornness and camel-malice.

Thomas Henry Huxley (1825–1895)
English biologist

Men will always opt for things that get finished
and stay that way—putting up screens, but not planning menus.

Jane O'Reilly

It is a conviction of mine that refined and perfect
domestic comfort is understood by men only.

Oliver Bell Bunce (1828–1884)
Welsh actor

Adam Was a First Draft.

1960s feminist button

It is funny that the two things most men are proudest of is the thing
that any man can do and doing does in the same way, that is being
drunk and being the father of their son.

Gertrude Stein (1874–1946)
American writer

MEN HAVE FEWER HEMORRHOIDS THAN WOMEN BECAUSE THEY'RE MORE PERFECT ASSHOLES.

Warren Farrell (b. 1943)
American psychologist and writer

What is a man? A miserable little pile of secrets.

André Malraux (1901–1976)
French writer

A man is one who loses his illusions first, his teeth second, and his follies last.

Helen Rowland (1875–1950)
American writer

Men are like tea—the real strength and goodness are not properly drawn until they have been in hot water.

Lillie Hitchcock Coit (1843–1929)

Our lives, she thought, summing up her sex in general, are an immolation; theirs, summing up his, are an escape.

Robert Speaight (1904–1976)
English actor and writer

Men are always ready to respect anything that bores them.

Marylin Monroe (1926–1962)
American actress

Men are very strange. When they wake up they want breakfast.
They don't eat candy in the morning like we do.
They want things like toast. I don't have these recipes.

Elayne Boosler (b. 1952)
American comedienne

*A man spends the first half of his life learning habits
that shorten the other half.*

Ann Landers (b. 1918)
American advice columnist

The members of the men's liberation movement are a kind of embarrassing vanguard, the first men anywhere on record to take a political stand based on the idea that what the women are saying is right—men are a bunch of lazy, selfish, horny, unhappy oppressors.

Barry Farrell

A feminist man is like a jumbo shrimp— neither makes any sense.

Cassandra Dans

Beware of the man who praises women's liberation; he is about to quit his job.

Erica Jong (b. 1942)
American writer and poet

The women's movement is rooted in the belief that we don't need men. All it will take is one natural disaster to prove how wrong that is. The only thing holding this culture together would be men of the working class.

Camille Paglia (b. 1946)
American writer

During the feminist revolution, the battle lines were again simple. It was easy to tell the enemy. . . . This is no longer strictly true. Some men are okay now. We're allowed to like them again. We still have to keep them in line, of course, but we no longer have to shoot them on sight.

Cynthia Heimel (b. 1947)
American writer and playwright

It may be that men are not equal in all respects, but they are all equally men.

Hugh Gaitskell (1906–1963)
English politician

What is woman? Only one of nature's agreeable blunders.

Hannah Cowley (1743–1809)
English playwright and poet

I've been a woman for fifty years, and I've never yet been able
to discover precisely what it is I am.

Jean Giraudoux (1882–1944)
French writer

Always begin with a woman by telling her that you don't understand women. You will be able to prove it to her satisfaction more certainly than anything else will ever tell her.

Don Marquis (1878–1937)
American writer

I want to make a policy statement.
I am unabashedly in favor of women.

Lyndon B. Johnson (1908–1973)
American president

Woman is a paradox who pleases when she puzzles,
and puzzles when she pleases.

Anonymous

To understand one woman is not necessarily
to understand any other woman.

John Stuart Mill (1806–1873)
English philosopher and economist

Women are fifty percent of the world, yet they always seem a novelty.

Christopher Morley (1890–1957)
American writer

If you're going to generalize about women,
you'll find yourself up to here in exceptions.

Dolores Hitchens (1907–1973)
Writer

Let me tell you something about women. They're selfish, they're
conniving, and if you don't care too much for dancing, you don't
need them at all.

from *Norman . . . Is That You?*

I believe in women. Men are just unsubstantiated rumors.

Erika Rittner
20th-century Canadian writer and broadcaster

195

Women are like tricks by sleight of hand,
Which, to admire, we should not understand.

William Congreve (1670–1729)
English dramatist

A woman's laugh is often her mating call.

from *Forever Female*

There are two ways to handle women . . .
nobody knows what they are.

from *Valley of the Sun*

A woman is like a teabag—only in hot water
do you realize how strong she is.

Nancy Reagan (b. 1921)
American First Lady

Never forget to assure a woman that she is unlike any other woman
in the world, which she will believe, after which you may proceed
to deal with her as with any other woman in the world.

D. B. Wyndham (1894–1969)
American writer

Do we know much about women? Do we? We don't. We know when they're happy, we know when they're crying, we know when they're pissed off. We just don't know what order those are gonna come at us.

Evan Davis

Women, being unique, you simply don't arrive anywhere by comparing them to men.

William F. Buckley Jr. (b. 1925)
American writer

Woman is not an equal but rather a sequel to man.

Dagobert D. Runes (1902–1982)
German-born American writer

WHEN WOMAN PLAYS WITH FIRE, MAN GETS BURNED.

from *Charlie Chan at the Olympics*

The woman who is known only through a man is known wrong.

Henry Brooks Adams (1838–1918)
American historian

Women complain about premenstrual syndrome,
but I think of it as the only time of the month I can be myself.

Roseanne (b. 1953)
American actress and comedienne

A woman's tongue is only three inches long,
but it can kill a man six feet high.

Japanese proverb

IF YOU DON'T THINK WOMEN ARE EXPLOSIVE, DROP ONE.

Gerald F. Lieberman (1923–1986)
American writer

The women's liberation warriors think they have something new,
but it's just their armies coming out of the hills. Sweet women ambushed
men always, at their cradles, in the kitchen, in the bedroom.

Mario Puzo (b. 1920)
American writer

Until Eve arrived, this was a man's world.

Richard Armour (1906–1989)
American educator and writer

Can you imagine a world without men?
No crime and lots of happy fat women.

Nicole Hollander

All dames are alike. They reach down your throat so they can grab your heart, they pull it out, they throw it on the floor and they step on it with their high heels. They spit on it. Then they slice it into little pieces, slam on a hunk of toast and serve it to you. And they expect you to say: Thanks honey, it's delicious.

from *Dead Men Don't Wear Plaid*

Women are like citadels. Some are taken by storm,
and others withstand a long and vigorous siege.

David Ainsworth

Women forgive injuries, but never slights.

Thomas Chandler Haliburton (1796–1865)
Canadian jurist and writer

It is rare that one can see in a little boy the promise of a man, but one can almost always see in a little girl the threat of a woman.

Alexandre Dumas (1824–1895)
French playwright

Women just want men who'll share your hopes and dreams.
If you don't we'll bitch at you until you die.

Stephanie Hodge

Women have two weapons—cosmetics and tears.

Napoleon Bonaparte (1769–1821)
French emperor

What I learned constructive about women is that no matter how old they get, always think of them the way they were on their best day they ever had.

Ernest Hemingway (1899–1961)
American writer

You can't reduce women to equality
because equality is a step down for most women.

Cindy Adams
20th-century American columnist

Women may be the one group that grows more radical with age.

Gloria Steinem (b. 1934)
American writer and feminist

The women behind the [women's liberation] movement want the same thing all group leaders want and have wanted through history: ego assuagement.

Robert J. Ringer (b. 1938)
American writer

These are very confusing times. For the first time in history a woman is expected to combine: intelligence with a sharp hairdo, a raised consciousness with high heels, and an open, non-sexist relationship with a tan guy who has a great bod.

Lynda Barry (b. 1956)
American writer and playwright

Women definitely go to maintenance extremes. It's amazing the way women take care of all the hair on their bodies. One of the great mysteries to me is the fact that a woman could pour hot wax on her legs, rip the hair out by the roots, and still be afraid of a spider.

Jerry Seinfeld (b. 1954)
American actor and comedian

There are two kinds of women: high maintenance and low maintenance.

from *When Harry Met Sally*

Being a woman is of special interest only to aspiring male transsexuals. To actual women it is merely a good excuse not to play football.

Fran Lebowitz (b. 1950)
American writer

Once women made it public that they could do things better than men, they were, of course, forced to do them. Now women have to be elected to political office, get jobs at offices at major corporations, and so on, instead of ruling the earth by batting their eyelashes the way they used to.

P. J. O'Rourke (b. 1947)
American writer and editor

Women have the feeling that since they didn't make the rules, the rules have nothing to do with them.

Diane Johnson (b. 1934)
American writer

Women [golfers] are handicapped by having boobs. It's not easy for them to keep their left arm straight, and that's one of the tenets of the game. Their boobs get in the way.

Ben Wright (b. 1947)
American sports commentator

Why are there so many women with fake fingernails, fake eyelashes and fake boobs complaining that there are no real men.

Gay Goodenough

Women never have young minds. They are born 3,000 years old.

Shelagh Delaney (b. 1939)
English playwright

Women are most fascinating between the ages of thirty-five and forty, after they have won a few races and know how to pace themselves. Since few women ever pass forty, maximum fascination can continue indefinitely.

Christian Dior (1905–1957)
French fashion designer

A woman's beauty lies, not in any exaggeration of the specialized zones, nor in any general harmony that could be worked out by means of the sectio aurea or a similar aesthetic superstition; but in the arabesque of the spine. The curve by which the back modulates into the buttocks. It is here that grace sits and rides a woman's body.

John Updike (b. 1932)
American writer

WOMEN ARE ONE OF LIFE'S GREAT MYSTERIES. TO SOME GUYS WOMEN ARE LIKE A JIGSAW PUZZLE WITH PIECES THAT JUST DON'T FIT. I THINK THE SOUL OF A WOMAN IS DARKER THAN A BACK ALLEY, AND MORE TANGLED THAN A TELEPHONE CORD, AND COLDER THAN AN ESKIMO PIE IN ANCHORAGE, BUT THOSE GUYS DON'T EVEN HAVE A CLUE. WHEN YOU KNOW WOMEN THE WAY I DO, YOU KNOW EXACTLY WHAT MAKES THEM TICK, WHAT MAKES THEM JIGGLE UP AND DOWN WHEN THEY WALK.—FROM *FATAL INSTINCT*

A woman, I always say, should be like a good suspense movie: the more left to the imagination, the more excitement there is. This should be her aim—to create suspense, to let a man discover things about her without her having to tell him.

Alfred Hitchcock (1899–1980)
English-born American director

Women should be obscene and not heard.

John Lennon (1940–1980)
English singer and songwriter

The entire being of a woman is a secret which should be kept.

Isak Dinesen [Karen Christence] (1885–1963)
Danish writer

Women are like elephants to me; I like to look at them, but I wouldn't want to own one.

from *Mississippi*

Women tell time by the body. They are like clocks. They are always fastened to the earth, listening for its small animal noises.

Anne Sexton (1928–1974)
American poet

Babes are like a bad song. Once you get 'em
stuck in your head you can't get 'em out again.

from *The Little Rascals*

Women are one of the Almighty's enigmas
to prove to men that He knows more than they do.

Ellen Glasgow (1873–1945)
American writer

God made man before woman to give him time to think of an answer for her first question.

Anonymous

The whole thing about women is, they lust to be misunderstood.

Will Rogers (1879–1935)
American writer and humorist

Women have a way of treating people more softly.
We treat souls with kid gloves.

Shirley Caesar

WOMEN ARE JUST LIKE CATS. TO WIN THEM, YOU MUST FIRST MAKE THEM PURR.

Sam "Sully" Gehring

A woman is like a slingshot: the greater the resistance,
the further you can get with 'em.

from *Leap of Faith*

Women find pallor seductive . . . Women are intrigued by a man
who looks like he's hiding dark secrets.

Conan O'Brien (b. 1963)
American talk show host

A woman talks to one man, looks at a second, and thinks of a third.

Bhartrihari
5th-century Indian poet and philosopher

*Women are divided into two classes: those who don't believe everything
their husbands tell them, and those who haven't any husbands.*

Anonymous

It is only women who can love and criticize in the same long look.

Maurice Hewlett (1861–1923)
English writer

Why can't a woman be more like a man?

from *My Fair Lady*

It's delightful to be a woman; but every man
thanks the Lord devoutly that he isn't one.

Olive Schreiner (1855–1920)
South African writer

A woman will always sacrifice herself if you give her the opportunity. It is her favorite form of self-indulgence.

William Somerset Maugham (1874–1965)
English writer

What a woman wants is what you're out of.
She wants more of a thing when it's scarce.

O. Henry [William Sydney Porter] (1862–1910)
American writer

There are only three things to be done with a woman. You can love her, you can suffer for her, or you can turn her into literature.

Lawrence Durrell (1912–1990)
English writer

We women are so much more sensible! When we tire of ourselves, we change the way we do our hair, or hire a new cook. Or redecorate the house. I suppose a man could do over his office, but he never thinks of anything so simple. No, dear, a man has only one escape from his old self—to see a different self in the mirror of some women's eyes.

from *The Women*

There are no women composers, never have been and possibly never will be.

Thomas Beecham (1879–1961)
English conductor

I just don't think women should be in the orchestra. They become men. Men treat them as equals; they even change their pants in front of them. I think it's terrible!

Zubin Mehta (b. 1936)
Indian conductor

Women are more likely to smile than men when delivering bad news.

Anonymous

When a man loses his temper, he is aggressive; I'm a pushy bitch.
A man is confident and authoritative; I'm conceited and power-mad.
Were I a man, I would be termed an excellent executive.

Leona Helmsley
20th-century American business executive

Women are like dreams—they are never the way
you would like to have them.

Luigi Pirandello (1867–1936)
Italian writer and playwright

I'M JUST A PERSON TRAPPED INSIDE A WOMAN'S BODY.

Elayne Boosler (b. 1952)
American comedienne

Women give us solace, but if it were not for women
we should never need solace.

Don Herold (1889–1966)
English writer

Every man knows that a woman has a dozen different ways
to make him happy, and a hundred to make him unhappy.

James Huneker (1860–1921)
American musician and critic

The prostitute is the only honest woman left in America.

Ti-Grace Atkinson (b. 1939)
American feminist

Woman would be more charming if one could fall
into her arms without falling into her hands.

Ambrose Bierce (1842–1914)
American writer

If women didn't exist, all the money in the world
would have no meaning.

Aristotle Onassis (1906–1975)
Greek shipping executive

Women have to make jokes about themselves,
laugh about themselves, because they have nothing to lose.

Agnès Varda (b. 1928)
French writer and director

Never try to impress a woman, because if you do
she'll expect you to keep up to the standard for the rest of your life.

W. C. Fields (1880–1946)
American comedian

Women are repeatedly accused of taking things personally.
I cannot see any other honest way of taking them.

Marya Mannes (1904–1990)
American writer

I STILL BELIEVE WOMEN ARE THE SUPERIOR SEX.

Jane Fonda (b. 1937)
American actress

When every unkind word about women has been said, we have still
to admit that they are nicer than men. They are more devoted,
more unselfish, and more emotionally sincere.

Cyril Connolly (1903–1974)
English critic and writer

Women are wiser than men
because they know less and understand more.

James Stephens (1892–1971)
American writer

One is not born a woman, one becomes one.

Simone de Beauvoir (1908–1986)
French writer

Women like silent men. They think they're listening.

Marcel Achard (1900–1974)
French playwright and director

Women are smarter than men because they listen.

Phil Donahue (b. 1935)
American talk show host

To a woman who knows her own mind men can only be a minor consideration.

Maria Bashkirtseff (1860–1884)
Russian diarist and painter

Being a woman is a terribly difficult trade,
since it consists principally of dealing with men.

Joseph Conrad (1857–1924)
English writer

Women can do any job men can and give birth while doing it.

Allan Heavey

It's harder to get a movie made about
an interesting woman than about a guy with a hangnail.

Nora Ephron (b. 1941)
American writer and screenwriter

Woman: the peg on which the wit hangs his jest, the preacher his text, the cynic his grouch, and the sinner his justification.

Helen Rowland (1875–1950)
American writer

I happen to be one who believes that if it wasn't for women,
us men would still be walking around in skin suits carrying clubs.

Ronald Reagan (b. 1911)
American president

Women get more unhappy the more they try to liberate themselves.

Brigitte Bardot (b. 1934)
French actress

To be a woman is something so strange, so confusing and
so complicated that only a woman could put up with it.

Sören Kierkegaard (1813–1855)
Danish philosopher and writer

Women treat us just as humanity treats its gods: they worship us but keep bothering us to do something for them.

from *The Picture of Dorian Gray*

All women are wonders because they reduce all men to the obvious.

from *Out of the Past*

Myself, I either want to be gratifying my nerve endings with TV, sex, a car or beer, or I want to be taking a nap. Women seem to have a more diffused agenda, involving all sorts of plans and people, and people getting together, and kids and families and more kids. And women, of course, never take naps.

Eric Bogosian (b. 1953)
American actor and playwright

I often want to cry. That is the only advantage women have over men—at least they can cry.

Jean Rhys (1894–1979)
English writer

I hate women because they always know where things are.

James Thurber (1894–1961)
American writer and humorist

Women are always eagerly on the lookout for any emotion.

Stendhal [E. Marle-Henri Beyle] (1783–1842)
French writer and critic

A real important thing is that, though I rely on my husband for love, I rely on myself for strength.

Dolly Parton (b. 1946)
American singer and actress

Men gossip less than women, but mean it.

Mignon McLaughlin
20th-century American writer and editor

Women are very much like religion:
we must take them on faith or go without them.

F. Marion Crawford (1854–1909)
Italian writer

According to the Bible, woman was the last thing God made. It must have been a Saturday night. Clearly, He was tired.

Alexandre Dumas (1824–1895)
French playwright

What do you think: women—a mistake? Or did he do it to us on purpose?

Jack Nicholson (b. 1937)
American actor

When women discovered the orgasm it was, combined with modern birth control, perhaps the biggest single nail in the coffin of male dominance.

Eva Figes (b. 1932)
English writer

Women are natural guerrillas. Scheming, we nestle into the enemy's bed, avoiding open warfare, watching the options, playing the odds.

Sally Kempton (b. 1943)
American writer

On one issue, at least, men and women agree: they both distrust women.

H. L. Mencken (1880–1956)
American writer and editor

Women observe subconsciously a thousand little details, without knowing they are doing so. Their subconscious mind adds these things together—and they call the result intuition.

Agatha Christie (1890–1976)
English writer

There are two sides to the story when men quarrel,
but at least a dozen when women quarrel.

Edgar Watson Howe (1853–1937)
American writer

Women give men the very gold in their lives. But they invariably want it back in small change.

Oscar Wilde (1854–1900)
Irish poet and playwright

Women's all right. The only place you can beat one
and not get thrown in jail is at the poker table.

from *The Biggest Game in Town*

When women kiss it always reminds one of prize-fighters shaking hands.

H. L. Mencken (1880–1956)
American writer and editor

Where women love each other,
men learn to smother their mutual dislike.

George Eliot [Mary Ann Evans] (1819–1880)
English writer

Men can't read men, but any woman can read a woman.

Charles Reade (1814–1884)
English writer and playwright

If a woman likes another woman, she's cordial.
If she doesn't like her, she's very cordial.

Irvin S. Cobb (1876–1944)
American writer

Few women are dumb enough to listen to reason.

William Feather (1889–1981)

Women don't really use more tag questions, do they?

Sally McConnell-Ginet

They all start out as Juliets and wind up as Lady Macbeths.

from *The Country Girl*

**These impossible women! How they do get around us!
The poet was right: can't live with them, or without them.**

Aristophanes (c. 450–338 B.C.)
Greek playwright

ABOUT THE AUTHOR

Ronald B. Shwartz is a lawyer and author of ***What Is Life? A Bowl of Cherries and Nearly 800 Other Answers*** and ***The 501 Best and Worst Things Ever Said About Marriage.*** He is a graduate of the University of Chicago Law School, where he served as Articles Editor of the ***University of Chicago Law Review.*** He is a member of the Massachusetts Academy of Trial Attorneys and has had essays and reviews published in the ***Wall Street Journal,*** the ***Nation,*** the ***Los Angeles Times,*** the ***American Spectator,*** the ***Sewanee Review,*** and a wide range of other prominent periodicals. In 1981 he was admitted to the National Book Critics Circle.